Bells, Two Tones & Sirens

34 years of Ambulance Stories

GORDON ENSTONE

authorHOUSE®

AuthorHouse™ UK Ltd.
500 Avebury Boulevard
Central Milton Keynes, MK9 2BE
www.authorhouse.co.uk
Phone: 08001974150

First published by AuthorHouse 12/10/2008

ISBN: 978-1-4389-3030-5 (sc)

Printed in the United States of America
Bloomington, Indiana

This book is printed on acid-free paper.

Contents

ACKNOWLEDGEMENTS

This book is an acknowledgement to all present and past Ambulance men and women throughout the whole of the UK including training staff, dispatch, call takers, stores and mechanics and all the backroom office staff that keep the ambulance staff ticking over.

Not enough has been done or likely to be done to acknowledge ambulance personnel for their hard work and dedication. Let know one underestimate the hard work by all ambulance staff, who over the years strived to achieve the standard of training to be where all Ambulance services are now. It was the ambulance staff who went on strike not only for extra pay but better training. They are the first medical aid on scene dealing with people who were dying in front of their very eyes. This was because of the very poor standard of training given to the staff, making them poorly equipped to do anything about it. It meant taking on the Government of the day, getting doctors to get us properly trained and the National Health Service to see the benefits in staffing and most importantly the patient.

They have not been awarded medals like the Fire Service and their Chief Officers, with the Queens Fire Medal. The police and

Chief Constables who dish out and receive Knighthoods, and the Queens police medal etc. Don't get me wrong some do deserve it. But throughout the Northern Ireland Conflict I didn't see one thing mentioned in the media about the ambulance staff who must have been under constant stress attending bombings and shootings on almost a daily basis, not knowing what dangers they were going into. But they did it, at what cost to their future health perhaps, that's something we will never find out.

One of my former Chief Ambulance officers Mr Norman Lakin worked hard to have erected a National Memorial for Ambulance Service Personnel, in memory of those who died and all those who served with them. This is located at the Millennium chapel of Peace and Forgiveness. The National Memorial Arboretum, Alrewas, Staffordshire.

I am for one, truly grateful to him for doing this. There are over eight hundred and names listed at the memorial and I knew well over thirty of the Men and Women who are remembered there.

I have been lucky in all my years in the service as an ambulance man, and even when I was going up the ladder of promotion to become a senior officer I worked with a great bunch of staff (their thoughts of me though, might be different)

My wife Valerie has had to put up with the phone ringing 24/7, going out at all times of the day and night, most of the time not knowing where or what I was called to. Even some times when I was not on call being called out not knowing when I might return home. On one occasion popped out to the chemist to buy some medicine for her, I did not return for nearly 5 hours.

Put upon again, in reading this book, over and over again, to check my spelling and grammar. Now I know why I had to have a personal assistant to help me with my administration.

Also my son Andrew who kept on at me to write this book and reminding me of some of the stories I had forgotten over the period of time, this was only him thinking he might get a bigger inheritance so he can go out and buy his sports car!

My two stepsons Michael for his I.T. help and Gary for the photographs that are used in this book.

I have tried to keep this as accurate as possible but as with all things if you don't keep a proper record of the events some of the details might be slightly understated, as I only kept a diary with headlines in! I was always being told off at school and later at college when I submitted my written work for marking, it came back marked, "Rather Terse"

INTRODUCTION

I joined the Hertfordshire Fire & Ambulance Brigade in December 1964 and because I was too young to drive the "Emergency Ambulance" as it was called then, I was put on to "Sitting Cars" now called Patients Transport Service (PTS), I was very pleased this happened to me. This was good training for me, as I hadn't had much experience in dealing with people, especially the elderly.

Progressing onto the emergency ambulance this was the most fulfilling job any one can do. Normal routine work one minute and then rushing off at speed to some incident that can be life or death to some one. It's a privilege to be allowed straight into peoples homes, and to learn about the most intimate details of their lives. To deliver a baby, or watch some one die in your arms because you hadn't been trained enough to deal with, or in a situation were there is nothing else you can do to help that person.

Promoted to Leading ambulance man (L/A), which was the first run on the ladder to being an officer. It involved having to do administration duties, making sure the rota is covered, check the pay sheets and train new staff, all this as well as still working on the ambulance.

Station officer was my next move, being in charge of the stores for the whole of the now Hertfordshire Ambulance Service. Ordering, supplying and auditing every bit of equipment for staff, ambulances and stations.

I became an operational Station officer, responsible for the day to day running of the ambulance station at St.Albans, with twenty two emergency staff, six patient transport staff and fourteen auxiliary staff. This was a new initiative to transport elderly patients from their home and transport them to the new geriatric day units being introduced by hospitals to look after the elderly during the day. They would work from 0800 to 1100 hrs and 1500 to 1730hrs. We had a variety of staff that would carry out various shifts during the week to fit in with their domestic arrangements. This was such a success that it spread out throughout Hertfordshire.

Dealing with staff issues and administration duties and attending incidents that needed an officer's presence.

Still moving on up, District superintendent, having overall responsibility for three stations, St. Albans, Hemel Hempstead and Berkhampstead ambulance stations and the two Station officers. This entailed more meetings with other health professionals, and the fire service who lease our stations to us. Ensuring that complaints are dealt with and any staff issues such as sickness, welfare of staff and disciplinary issues are dealt with and Health & Safety legislation that was now coming on stream. In this year of 1987 I dealt with forty two complaints, at the time we were conveying an average 390 patients a day out of those complaints only 19 were justified. Ten of these were caused by the hospital not informing us that the patients were deceased, we would be calling at the house to convey the patient to hospital and on one occasion at the same time as the Hearse. This caused more distress to the family.

The complaint was upheld in favour of the complainant! I still cannot fathom that one out, even today.

Nearly there, at the top but not quite though! Divisional officer, my responsibility was for the west side of Hertfordshire. We used to say West is best! it was the busiest side of the county for all patient movements, and dealing with emergency calls.

Altogether I had responsibility for seven stations Borehamwood, Garston, Watford, Rickmansworth, Berkhampstead, Hemel Hempstead and St. Albans, 179 staff. As with the other promotions, these were operational so I had a responsibility to be on call and to deal with all matters whether that was to attend as a liaison officer at an entrapment at a RTA, fire situation or to be in attendance for crews making statements to the police re an incident they might have dealt with. Making sure the wheels kept on turning. Attending meetings with senior officers making sure budgets are adhered to, meeting with control managers. Also that the shift cover of staff to provide ambulances is kept to. Ensure ORCON is met and dealing with the trade union stewards, health and Safety issues, meetings with various hospital, administrators and doctors.

After reorganisation and the amalgamation with Bedfordshire ambulance service we became the Bedfordshire and Hertfordshire ambulance and Paramedic Service, BHAPS for short or as some staff used to say Be haps we would or Be haps we wouldn't. The boundaries changed after a small period of time, and then it was down to two of us to become Divisional commanders each taking half of Hertfordshire and Bedfordshire each. Then my opposite number took over the running of our very good training school. That meant I became Assistant Director of operations with responsibility of the control centre as well as all the operational stations in both counties. Dealing with a budget of £10.million for salaries, equipment, laundry and other bits and pieces. This was the best time in the service dealing with all the problems and some brilliant times as well. I had the support of my Director Bob Cass, and operational officers, Dave Guy, Tony Egan, Bob Anderson, Graham Calcott, Tim Bowditch and Bob Clarke the emergency planning officer. It was more political with a small "p" with budgets at the top of the agenda.

For the last seven months in the service responsible for running the resources unit. So in all those 34 years I had been with 6 different employers but had not moved outside my county. The biggest difference to happen to the ambulance service was when it became a NHS Trust and that's when the whole of the National Health Service became a business. Everything then was lead by money no patient moved unless we knew where the money was coming from to pay for the journey. That led to some soul searching for the paymasters! That's the ambulance service for you. The only thing that is constant in the ambulance service is change.

These short stories are from my 34 years experience and odd ones from my staff who would come back from a job, and they would relate to me, because they were different from the normal run of the mill incidents.

CHAPTER 1:
Starting off on my road to employment

On leaving school I started work at De Havilland (D H) at Leavesden near Watford as a pre-apprentice; I always wanted to be an aero engine fitter. I always had an interest in aeroplanes. One of my uncles let me work on his cars, stripping the engine, and putting it together again. I also helped out with several mates cars as well. So I thought I could combine the two interests. I had been working on the shop floor for about four months running errands for everybody really, when I was invited to D. H. main office in Edgware. I went to be interviewed again having already been interviewed once on entering D.H. by a different selection board to see what talent, if any I had to be selected for an apprenticeship. I was informed after about three weeks of waiting, that I would only be offered a position as a sheet metal worker. This didn't appeal to me at all, so being a young and know it all I said no thanks, I will go else where, the trouble was I didn't know where else where was.

I ended up working for a printing company, only half a mile from my house in St. Albans which was owned and run by the

Salvation Army. The main work was printing the War Cry and Bibles and quite a few other things as well. I worked in the postal department, my boss said I was being wasted in here, and told me there was a vacancy on the top floor in the accounts office and I should apply for it.

Off I went to train in accounts. The only fun there was the elderly office clerk, she would return from lunch and as the sun beat down through the office window she would nod off to sleep! But unfortunately for her she had the only pencil sharpener in the office the old handle type ones, yes you guessed, I would walk quietly over to her desk put my pencil in and wind with all my might and she would wake up with such a start!

I was in the hairdressers the barber who had known me since I was a kid, asked how I was getting on in my new job, big mistake. I said the new Colonel in charge of the works was a bit of a pratt and I waffled on for a bit about him. Then a person who was only a few years younger than me got out the chair, as he was being brushed down by the barber he turned, looked at me and said. 'You are talking about my father!'

Oops!

So after a short while I left and went to work for Thomas De La Rue another printing firm. They printed Bank notes, cheque books and all kinds of security printing. I was getting fed up with working indoors going to college taking exams in accounting .The last straw came when at the end of each month we had to do trail balances to give to the directors who came up from London to see how the factory was doing . Having been in work from 0600hrs it was getting hot in the office so I took my jacket off, well you would think that I was committing witch craft. The Chief Accountant came out of his office and said

'Gordon it would not look good if any of the workers came up from the shop floor and saw you with your jacket off, and in your shirt sleeves as well'

Well you guessed I didn't stay long after that, and having had a long yearning to work in the ambulance service after being taken to hospital when I was a small boy by an ambulance, I thought well I will have a year of doing that, and then I will go back into accounting

It all started when I had an interview with two ambulance officers who would later become my Station Officer and District Superintendent. I was taken out in a Bedford C.A. sitting car; they are used for taking out patients to hospital. The driving test lasted about twenty minutes; the usual things reverse up a side street, do a three point turn. Having passed that successfully, (well I didn't hit anything) I was taken back to the office to have a dictation test. Having proved that I could write and spell and understand English, to be honest I don't think they could talk much slower for me to write it all down so that was all ok. Then the questions

Why do you want to be an ambulance man? Do you think you will stay with us, or are you just waiting to move on to be an accountant? I see on your application form you are a Flag Marshall at Brands Hatch motor circuit, so are you just joining us to race around with blue lights on.

I must have answered their questions to their satisfaction or they were that desperate they took me on any way. And when I did arrive on the station for the first time to start my employment, I found out I was right, they were that desperate they would have taking any one on at the time!

The officers told me that if I had been successful I would hear from them after I had a medical examination by our Brigade doctor. That appointment came three weeks after the interview. Doctors like all doctors; were kind, sympathetic, but awfully thorough. The tests came, can you touch your toes, and can you read the eye chart. Hold your breath for about 10 minutes well that's how long it seemed as I nearly turned blue, stand on one leg and touch your nose all at the same time. Of course the last thing I had to do was cough as he delved into my underpants!

Then nothing for about four weeks, thinking to myself, had I failed the medical? Then on a Thursday evening at around 1930hrs a knock came at the door. I opened the door and an ambulance was outside my house, an ambulance man gave me a letter with out saying anything apart from good evening, good bye! It said I had been successful in being selected for joining the Hertfordshire Fire and Ambulance Brigade. I was to report to the St Albans Fire and ambulance station the next morning at eight a clock. Blow me I thought, left it a bit late to tell people what is happening, but as my time went on in the service this was going to be nothing unusual.

Well I thought if I don't like it, its only a year out of my life, and the money was going to be crap. At £9.50 per week working on the ambulance compared to £17.50 per week in accounts, you can see my reasoning.

And that ONE year lasted 34 years and I enjoyed every minute of it, I would recommend this job to anybody who enjoys dealing with people and the excitement of no two jobs being the same or what is coming next.

CHAPTER 2:
The Basics

Friday morning I walked from my home to the station in the middle of the city centre in St. Albans. Not really knowing what I had let myself in for or what to expect on my first day. I thought, the walk would steady my nerves.

This station was due for closure in a month's time. It was situated in the centre of St. Albans and had been built really for only two fire engines many years before and was becoming too small for the fire engines as well as the ambulances. I was met by the station officer who welcomed me and told me what would happen during the coming day.

He also told me that you do not call fire engines, fire engines they are called fire appliances!

Then we went off in his car to the Fire and Ambulance Headquarters at Hertford so that all the administration could take place. I handed over my P45 filled in forms re my next of kin, and given all the documentations on pay and conditions.

Off to Brigade County Supplies at Hatfield. I was issued with my uniform one pair of shoes, a pair of Wellingtons, cap and cap badge, two pairs of trousers, tunic, great coat, 2 x ties, 2 x shirts with no collars, 4 x collars and collar studs. I also got one Mac, one pair of black leather gloves, oh I nearly forgot three pairs of black socks, I was amazed as we loaded all stuff into the station officer's car. Right he said we will go and dump this lot off at your home and go back to the station. I arrived home and unloaded this mountain of clothing in the front room,

My mum said, 'Where an earth are you going to put this lot?'

We left her to it, and went back to the station for me to ride out on ambulance with two "Old Boys" for the rest of the day, to see how things happened out on the road. Nothing happened during the rest of that day on the ambulance I was on. So at five o'clock I was told I could go home and report back at 0800hrs on Monday.

Monday arrived and I walked to work in my new uniform as proud as punch, but I was not so sure about the cap. I am not a hat type person and not wearing a cap was going to get me into trouble on more than one occasion during my years of service.

I was told I would not be attending training school until the New Year, so in the meantime I was sent out in a sitting car to see what I would have to contend with. The driver was an old boy, and in those days ambulance men did all sitting car work as well as the emergency work on the ambulances, it was built into their shift rota. As I was still under 21, I was not old enough to drive the emergency ambulances so that's why I was to be placed onto sitting cars which were Bedford C/A with six seats.

I attended our training school at Headquarters in Hertford along with twelve other new recruits who would be based around various ambulance stations in Hertfordshire. We were told that this course would last for two weeks, I thought there would be an intense training in first aid, and all the workings of the human body, well that was my first big mistake and a shock in joining the ambulance brigade.

I thought this is where I was going to learn about first aid, anatomy and all the necessary learning to be an ambulance man. Well, no, because we were a Fire & Ambulance Brigade. We learnt how the service was run, we soon found out the Fire service held the purse strings, and told our officer what to do as well, even though the good ones would only give them lip service. We learnt how to operate the radio, the forms we had to fill in, (nothing like the patient report forms that have to be filled in now) just a one line, time of call, miles covered, patient name, address of patient, and place of incident!

The biggest period of time was allocated to Civil Defence! What to do if the "H" bomb was dropped, the most likely locations where they would be dropped in the U.K. And one of those locations was in Hertfordshire! This was the period of the three minute warning, but up to three weeks notice for the top brass, to disappear into their underground bunkers. Whilst the rest of us in the country stayed in their house sheltering under the stairs, as per the pamphlet we all had delivered through every body's door. God knows what the people in bungalows done, phone a friend! Not in those days, not many people had telephones.

The officer went onto explain the number of injured and dead we would have to deal with, all the blast injuries and radiation burns and the amount of radiation we might encounter. I said to the officer that I thought this was purely academic as we would not be around to be of any help if it did happen. He didn't think much of what I said, in fact it went down like a lead balloon. But he still went on to explain that we would be issued with meters to see if the radiation was safe enough to go outside. I started to giggle at this, and within minutes I had the whole class laughing. Now the lecturer being an ex military man was not amused and the more he went on, I had to bite into my lip to stop my laughter. I was glad when break came because the pain from biting the inside of my lip was bloody sore.

What I thought would take up most of the time learning anatomy was only the basics, this is the heart this is what it does etc., I remember the resuscitation method at the time was the Holgar Neilson method, (don't even bother knowing about it)

Basically we just used a triangular bandage, tie him/her up in triangular bandages and rush of to hospital. Otherwise known as scoop and run. (And in some cases that should be done now) We were told it doesn't matter how good the hospital is or how good the doctors were, if we took the patient in dead they were going to remain dead. But if took them in with some kind of life then the doctors had a fighting chance for them to work on.

There were seventeen ambulance stations all attached to fire stations for the whole of Hertfordshire. Within three years that figure was reduced to fourteen stations, and not one protest was uttered by the public. When it came to closing down fire stations all hell was let loose by the general public strange! Or was I becoming a cynic already against the sacred cow of the fire service?

We were also told how some of the stations were manned. Royston and Buntingford only did 0700/1500Hour and 1500/2300 shifts. When the late shift went off duty they would be on call from home. If a call came in within their area they had a bell in their house and they would get called out by control by this method. They would have to then get to the ambulance station to pick up the ambulance and then proceed onto the call. Watford and Garston Stations on a Friday and Saturday night would be manned by St. John Volunteers.

At the end of this "Intensive Training" we all had a little exam to make sure some of it went in our little heads.

So when were we going to learn our first aid skill?, well that was to come later when a 6 week course, one evening per week consisting of two hours was run by the St. John ambulance brigade but only when one became available. This course was paid for by the Ambulance Brigade and we would receive extra pay for passing this course, an extra 50p a week! So off we went to learn our first aid skills to be taught by these volunteers, training alongside housewives or anyone else who wanted a first aid certificate.

Working on the sitting cars I learnt a great deal, and even though I would eventually go on to the emergency ambulance, all the staff still drove the sitting cars either on overtime or covered by the rota system we worked. When we were not on emergencies we carried the out patients (OPD) on the emergency ambulance, these were the non walking OPD it also made sure we didn't sit around on the station getting in the way of the firemen who would be playing volley ball or polishing their fire appliances.

This often caused control problems trying to find an ambulance to attend any incidents, we only had the two ambulances during the day for our city and these could be filled up with OPD. The control staff would be scratching around trying to get an ambulance to attend some incident or other, and asking you to unload your patients as quickly as possible.

I remember one of our regular patients we used to pick up was from a local convent. This Nun would always complain that the ambulance was stuffy and she wanted the window pulled down, so my crew mate would say 'Put your boot down to the hospital as fast as you can'

She would hang onto her habit like mad as the wind flew in through the open window at a rate of knots, but she would always say, when she alighted from the ambulance,

'That's fine driver, nice drop of Gods fine air!'

I enjoyed my time on the sitting cars it gave me a great insight into patients needs and I learnt where all the hospitals were, we also had to go into London every day and that greatly helped me to find all the short cuts around London.

Meeting up with these elderly people who would talk about their life history because most of the time we were the only people they saw. Making sure they had their keys, appointment card and enough money for a cuppa tea. I knew the odd ambulance man who would leave his hat on the front of the cab floor so when the patient got in or out of the sitting car they would drop the odd coin in it; enough was gathered for him to get tea and sandwiches all day! Even though I lived with my mum, brother, grandma and granddad I still needed those first few months dealing with mostly elderly people. In fact I believe it should be the only way that new recruits should be allowed into the ambulance service. Coming in through the Patient Transport is a great way of knowing if it's going to be the right kind of job for them, I can hear staff shouting, you old git! Get with it.

One day whilst going through our city of St. Albans there was a policeman standing at the large crossroads and this elderly patient saying,

'I don't know, they take on anybody nowadays'

I didn't have a clue what she was on about. So I asked her what she said,

She replied, 'Didn't you see that policeman on the corner he's wearing a hearing aid, such a shame they can't find some one who could be more suitable'.

So politely I said no I hadn't noticed, but I knew the police had just been issued with new hand sets for that era and they all had ear pieces they wore or they couldn't hear a word.

Also just inside the door of these sitting cars was a cupboard, on the top of this (which was only three foot high) were our service radios which were about the size of a small suitcase. As the patients got in through the side of the ambulance door they normally pulled themselves up on this to get into the ambulance, one elderly lady asked

'What is this thing on here?'

I replied 'It's a radio,'

'Oh shut that off' she said 'I can't stand all that banging music they play nowadays!'

I was called back to base one day to see my station officer and thought, What have I done now? Because nine times out of ten, you never saw the station officer only to get a bollocking. As I arrived at the station he met me in the yard and said,

'You have a special job!'

Oh good I thought a change, this sounds exciting, it was to go the local police station, and convey a patient to a mental prison, sorry hospital. On arrival at the police station I was told to back right up to cell doors. Whereupon out walked a little bedraggled man in his late forties handcuffed to a police sergeant, they sat down in the sitting car and off we went. For the whole journey not a word was spoken by me the patient or the sergeant so it was quite strange really something I hadn't been used to in my short experience.

On arrival at the prison hospital I found the right ward, rung the bell and eventually the door opened and out came two burley prison officers, sorry mental health nurses, in prison officer's uniform.

We walked into the ward and the sergeant undid the handcuffs, and before the sergeant had time to hand over this man, these two men. They got hold of this little man pushed him to the floor and proceeded to kick him up and down the very highly polished parquet floor! Then they picked him up.

And said 'that's for fuck all, you do anything out of turn and that's the least you can expect.'

I walked out of that place and as I turned to the sergeant I noticed he was as shocked at this as I was.

And I said 'What an earth had this man done to deserve that'

I was even more shocked at his reply,

'He had been arrested for walking through the High street (St. Albans) flashing and exposing himself for about 3 minutes before he was arrested'.

I drove back with the sergeant as quiet as we went up and I could tell he was not impressed either, I had never seen anything as unwarranted as this attack.

I believe most people in the world have heard of this great man, Dr Yacoub, what an outstanding heart surgeon. One night at around 0100 hrs, the phone rang into our control room where we used to sit if we were bored, it was Harefield hospital OPD, ringing to say that they had three patients who were ready to be taken to their home addresses. The controller was surprised at such a late hour. Dr Yacoub had just finished his outpatient clinic, had been tied up in surgery all afternoon and most of the night but said he would still do his outpatients after surgery if the patients didn't mind waiting!

Our problem was we only had the accident ambulances on at that time in the morning and very few of them as well. The patients didn't mind a bit, it was even longer before these patients got home, and I think the last patient got home around 0430hrs, what an amazing Doctor.

On the sitting cars we always started our shift at 0800, I usually got in at 0745 and one day was met by the station officer rushing around telling me to get into my vehicle immediately and go to the rear of Handly Page airfield near Radlett where a train was on fire where there was believed to be many casualties. This was my first emergency call, only one problem, our "cars" were not equipped with blue lights or bells. I raced off, hand pressing down on the road horn, headlights on thinking this is great. Car drivers were not taking any notice of me, I might as well been flying to the moon, but to be honest they didn't always move out of the way for emergency ambulance either. The bells on the ambulances had to compete with more and more radios being fitted into private cars and people could not hear us, but bells had reached the end of their shelf life, but that's another story.

On arrival at this incident there were fire service vehicles by the tens, police by the tens and a couple of ambulances. It appears that this train was a new type of multi carriage diesel which had caught fire while travelling at around 70mph. It was the morning rush hour and it was packed full of passengers. The fire officer in charge told me to round up as many walking patients as I could find and convey them to the hospital. In all I did two trips conveying 12 patients. The patient's injuries ranged from those who had been overcome with smoke and cuts and abrasions, some had jumped out of the train when it was slowing down. Its not until you are up close to trains standing on the track that you realise how high up they are, and these patients had jumped from some height.

Strange thing about a month or two later the same thing happened, nearer to our station so I didn't have as far to travel to the incident, it was only a mile from the station so not so exciting or as many casualties this time. It turned out that the train was a similar make and model as the other train fire I had been to previously. British Rail found the problem that had started these fires which affected every type of this model. From then on we had no more calls

Even though my time on the sitting cars was only for a few months during that time I had two unusual incidents involving the ambulance. The first time it happened to me I was bringing a patient from Hertford to St. Albans when this clonking noise started coming from the back end of the ambulance. I was approaching Brigade Workshops at Hatfield and called control on the radio and told them my plight and my intentions to call into brigade workshops and as it was a Saturday morning I knew some one would be working. I was about 200yards when the back wheel of the ambulance came off! It overtook me as I was only doing about 15mph so the damage was not bad. The patient was not impressed as she had to get home to cook her husband's dinner, and all she wanted to know was when she would get home. I had to fill in an accident report and give the reason why I hadn't stopped straight away to investigate the noise. My reply was that, as I wasn't trained as a mechanic I would not know what to look for anyway.

About two months later I was driving through Bricket Wood with two patients on board, I was driving a different sitting car when the same noise started again from the back of the ambulance. I thought, I know that sound, so this time I stopped got out of the vehicle and checked the back wheel and sure enough the wheel was hanging off! I called up control and told them what's happened. The station officer turns up with the mobile mechanic.

I said 'well I did what you wanted now what?'

'Well', he said 'I will submit a report about your problem'.

I replied, 'It's not my problem it's Vauxhalls they make the things'.

He was not impressed with me again at my reply.

Not long after that the night crews had to check the wheel nuts on every ambulance to ensure the problems never happened again. Which upset the fireman because at 2300hrs they went to bed apart from those that sat at the bar drinking until the early hours. So us poor ambulance bods used to make as much noise as possible in taking the wheel caps off as they hit the tile floor.

Then my time came as I was now twenty one years of age and could go onto the emergency ambulance. Thankfully you were always put on with an experienced member of staff who guides you through each job with gestures that hopefully were not too apparent to the patient that showed you were complete novices.

Our sparsely equipped ambulances were Bedford 'J' the new kid on the block, which were replacing the Daimler's, the great old work horse with its pre-select gear box, and a great ride in the back for the patient, and stuck to road like glue. It was as big as a battle ship big long nose plenty of room in the back. No power steering and the wooden stretcher weighed a ton. You soon built up muscles and when you put a patient on the stretcher you got muscles on muscles.

Just like the Daimler the Bedford 'J' could take two stretchers and the best thing about it was the permanent stretcher was made of aluminium what a relief. The equipment was a first aid satchel containing triangular bandages, dressings cotton wool rolls, smelling salts, constrictive bandage made out of rubber and safety pins, and a bottle of Sal Voliatle. A carry chair the most important piece of equipment carried on the ambulance. It was the only way of removing patients from houses. One small oxygen bottle plenty of blankets, hot water bottles, pillows, incontinent pads by the lorry load, bucket to put bits and pieces in wooden splints in varying lengths, vomit bowls. We younger members tried to get the patients to vomit in our caps as we didn't like wearing them.

The stretcher was laid out in a special way so as soon as you laid a patient on it you could wrap them up without wasting time. The Bedford 'J' was not as long as the Daimler but it was taller so you could stand up in the back of the ambulance.

One thing I soon learnt about being an ambulance man was how inadequate our training was going to be in dealing with what I was going to come across.

We are not social workers but have resolved some serious social problems.

We were not midwifes but have to deliver babies in some strange places.

We were not mental health workers but have to deal with mental health problems.

We were not doctors but are expected to sustain life until handed over to doctors.

We were under valued by successive governments.

We had to work until we have reached the age of 65 not so for the other emergency services.

An ambulance man attends 331 999 calls per ambulance man per year.

A Fireman attends four 999 calls per year.

A Policeman attends 25 calls per year.

These figures relate to a survey carried out in 1967

In 1966 there was a national dispute involving the ambulance service, we were demanding a separate pay scale from other local authority workers but also our main gripe was the lack of training. The Government, after some time gave us a slight pay rise. More importantly they gave us the most important demand we wanted; an investigation by a Doctor Millar to see what improvements could be brought in to save peoples lives in better training techniques. He recommended a far longer training period, and to be trained by our own ambulance staff. The initial batch of staff had to be trained by doctors, and then that was spread out through out the rest of the counties ambulance services. We were issued with a laurel leaf badge to be placed on our left arm to show we had been properly trained in the new modern methods at the time. This badge became known as the Millar badge.

I had to attend the school in Essex to acquire my Millar Badge, it was a good 3 week course and even though I had now been an ambulance man for four years I still learnt new techniques. One pair of ambulance men had come from, Great Yarmouth in Norfolk which was a separate ambulance service from the Norfolk ambulance service. One of them had been a rear gunner on Lancaster bombers during WW11. When it got to the day we had to take our test either written or practical he was a bag of nerves, which surprised me. There was this man who was a real life hero, and had been shot at every night, suffered burns and had to bale out, but was under stress when it came to the exam. Perhaps looking back a few years later I should not have been surprised. These two men were a great laugh during the course, because if an instructor said this bit of equipment does this,

They would say in their Norfolk accent 'We don't have that, pillows we have to bring in cushions from home! Those blankets they look good we get ours from jumble sales but they don't seem to last long!'

When it came for my practical exam, we would take it in turns to be an injured person, but we made sure we would help each other to pass the exam. I was told with another ambulance man, that we were attending a situation in a pub where there had been a fight. As we walked into the room, there was one man on the floor and one man holding on to the bar. I went to the man on the floor and started talking to him, making sure the examiner could hear me.

'Hello sir my name is Gordon I am here to help you what's the problem?'

He replied 'I think I am having a heart attack'"

'Ok sir don't worry we will sort you out' I thought, Funny some bloody fight this is.

'No, no I am really having a heart attack'

'Yes that's ok sir I believe you, I will put you on oxygen and then we will get you off to hospital soon'

Once he again he insisted 'No, no I am really having a heart attack',

I felt like saying to him stop pissing about, I am playing the game here I haven't forgotten anything. Then as I took his pulse it was very erratic to say the least,

I said to the examiner 'I think he's right!'

The examiner came over some what puzzled and said "I told him that for the exam he was to have been stabbed by a knife"

The doctor came in and found that my fellow student was really having a panic attack and not a heart attack. I thought he was being a fly in the ointment in stopping me from passing my test, and when he felt better later, we all had a great laugh. Yes I did pass my practical exam.

Also we had to carry out two weeks observing in our local hospital. We saw operations being carried out, and as if we didn't know already what happened in the casualty department. I observed four operations, two hip replacements an appendectomy and the removal of a tumour of the breast. We were on call in case any babies were born, so we could see how a delivery should be carried out properly. I never heard of one person being called to see a baby being delivered. The midwives were to ask the mothers to be if they would allow us into the delivery suite to see a birth, but I honestly believed that no midwife asked any of the mothers and that's why we never got to see one.

CHAPTER 3:
Murders

It might seem strange or just one of those things, but I only dealt with two murders whilst I was in the Hertfordshire Ambulance Service, but as soon as we amalgamated with the Bedfordshire Ambulance Services I attended as many in two months as I had in the previous 26years, all of those happened in Luton!

In my experience most murders turned out to members of the same family.

We were called to a small lane near Shenley in the middle of nowhere to a car fire, we were informed that the caller was unsure if anybody was inside the car. On arrival the fire had burnt itself out, and there appeared to be a person in the back seat with what looked like a load of egg boxes. A policeman said he thought this could be a suicide as there was a body inside. My colleague and I checked the car and I noticed blood on the boot lid of the car which I thought was strange.

I said to the policeman, 'how could this be suicide if there was blood on the outside of the car'

We told him, we would leave the body for him to look after as the person was well and truly dead, even though we were not allowed to say this. Also as it was out of the public gaze and in a very narrow lane, telling the policeman over to you and goodnight, we left him to it. We later learnt the policeman was commended for his observation of the blood on the car as it turned out to be a murder.

It turned out that the deceased was a male and his wife was having an affair, and she got her boyfriend and his mate to knock him off. As he arrived home he was attacked outside his house with a hammer, then bundled into the car, taken to this location, propped up in the back seat, then they set it alight and off they went.

The one murder that really stick in my mind was a shooting in Luton; the Station Officer and I attended a call to a person shot, and the person, who had carried out the shooting had driven off.

On arrival there was a young man kneeling over a young girl and there was an empty push chair next to them. The young girl had been shot in the head and was obviously dead lying in a big pool of blood. This had happened in broad day light in a street not far from the main town centre. We took the man away from the ladies body so we could ask him what had happened.

He was in a very shocked condition. He managed to tell us that he was walking along the road with his girl friend pushing the push chair with their baby, when this van suddenly stopped, and a man got out, as he approached us he produced a gun and shot his girlfriend and then grabbed the baby out of the pram and just threw the baby into the back of the van and drove off!.

As Bob and I were listening to what he was telling us I was truly shocked by this. If there is anything that's disturbs me in the job is children being injured in any way. The police then arrived and took over the scene, and we left the young man in hands of the police who were going to look after him.

I was going on holiday the next day and I could not stop thinking about this poor baby and what would happen to it. After a couple of days they found the baby having been shot to pieces by a shotgun in a lane a few miles away from where the baby had been snatched.

It turned out to be the girl's former boyfriend who carried out this wicked deed and he was caught by the police and sentenced to imprisonment. I remember when he was appearing at Crown Court in Luton the convoys of police cars that escorted the prison van off the motorway, as they used to go past our ambulance station to get to the Court.

Carrying on with the family theme of murders, called by Control to a house in Luton saying a woman had been stabbed police enroute. On arrival a female was on the kitchen floor in a big pool of blood all over the kitchen and there was this man leaning against the fridge.

'I fucking told her, if she brought anything, using the credit card again, I would fucking kill her'.

It was her husband and it appeared she had not taken heed of what he had told her. He went on to say as he waved the visa statement in his hand, that she had used the credit card FORTY NINE times so he stabbed her FORTY NINE times.

Well he said 'I told her not to do it, it's her own fault, let her try using the fucking thing now the fucking cow!'

He was as cool as a cucumber and was not perturbed at all by what he had done even after the police arrested him. He just walked off to the police car as though he was going out to the shops.

A Murder that upset me and got me throwing my teddy out of the pram, but it didn't get me anywhere during or after the event. I was at home in the evening with my wife and daughter Nicola, who was in the ambulance service on Patient transport service (PTS). The phone rang and it was control asking me to attend some kind of incident in a house in Hemel Hempstead involving children, the call was still coming in and I would be passed more details enroute. This is quite a normal practice when our controllers are not quite sure themselves as to the kind of call that's coming in.

This could be either the caller had not been precise in the details passed over the phone or other agencies like the police are still passing information to them. Whilst I was enroute the first ambulance had arrived on scene, ascertained that a lady had locked herself in her flat with a child, but one child was out of the flat with serious head injuries.

They asked for a further ambulance, and as the police were on scene they said they were leaving the scene for the A&E. department and to have a Doctor standing by because of the seriousness of the injury to the child. On my arrival at the scene I found a police Inspector that I could liaise with. I needed to make sure I had the enough resources. I must say that in all my time in the ambulance service this Inspector and one other police man, were the most uncooperative I have ever come across. On the whole we in the ambulance service, we enjoyed a great working relationship with the police far better than with the Fire service.

He told me that the lady inside the flat had gone into a "Raving mad state" battered the first child, which had got out of the flat unsure how. Then locked herself into the flat and turned the gas taps on. There was another child in the flat and he went on to say that he had called the fire service and the gas board to come so they could turn the gas off before he would allow anybody to go anywhere near the flat. I suggested to him about going into the flat now before the build up of gas as it wouldn't do any harm to any of us or to the people inside. Being natural gas it would not be poisonous to us but the longer we waited the more volatile it would become and could explode.

He would not agree, so I reminded him of the incident in Kent where a woman had been shot and the person who did it was dead, but still the police would not go into the house although she was still alive talking to police on the phone, but died before they went in. I was concerned the same thing was going to happen to this child, but he still would not risk it.

I was not at all happy with this situation and I went to my car and phoned the control officer to bring her up to speed. In the mean time the second ambulance had arrived as well as the Fire service and us were just waiting for the gas board to arrive, which I must say they came very quickly indeed, but so did the press and TV reporters. I was getting quite annoyed at this situation, and made my feelings known to the inspector again, which went in one ear and straight out the other side.

Then all of a sudden a call came from the flat which I found out to be CID officers, they had broken into the flat. I rushed into the flat with my crew and everybody else as the lady was being pulled out of the flat by police officers. I went straight down the hallway to see if I could find the other child, the place was very Spartan and very messy, I looked under the rubbish to look for this child and then a shout came from a police officer who had found the child in the bathroom in a bath full of water.

Everybody was then ordered out of the flat, I intervened and said no I want my paramedic to check this child out, to see if the child could be resusitated, reluctantly they agreed to this. But unfortunately the child was dead as he had sustained other injuries as well.

After the incident I went to the hospital to meet up with first crew members to talk through this very sad incident I went home angry and upset over this incident not knowing if an earlier intervention would have helped or not. I gave it a day or two, so I could ring the police Inspector without anger in my voice and asked for a meeting to debrief this incident. He said he would arrange it but after ringing him up again I had no response from this officer so I felt I never had a satisfactory ending to this story.

As I spend more time in the service I have failed to understand why people carry out such dreadful deeds against their partners surely a divorce is much easier. Well for some people perhaps, even though mine had its problems re-money issues I could not have murdered her!. As another call comes in for someone who won't get out of bed, Garston a fire in a flat person burnt. On arrival the crew were sent into a bedroom by a woman where a man was lying in bed on fire, the fire service was there at the same time and quickly extinguished the fire.

The woman then started shouting saying,

'He wouldn't get out of bed to go work. I am fucking well fed up with it, always calling him to get up every morning. Now the fucking bastard won't be late any more, I have poured paraffin over him and lit a match to make him move off his fucking arse.'

Well she was right about one thing he wouldn't be late ever again. He later died in hospital from the burns he sustained.

A crew came into my office, having just dealt with another murder involving family members. It appears that they were called to a stabbing between two brothers. The brothers had been sorting out free newspapers for delivery, and an argument broke out between them. One of them didn't want to do one particular area. As the arguing got more and more heated it lead to one of the brothers stabbing the other one with the knife they were using to cut the string, to tie the newspapers up with. The crew said the young male was dead on their arrival at the scene, they were both in there early twenties. It appeared that the parents were not that surprised that this outcome, as they were always fighting between each other!

Flitwick is a small village in a small country lane turned out to be a bit more than it seemed, it was thought to be an RTA, car into a railway bridge, persons trapped. A car had gone into a railway bridge support, on our arrival there were two people in the car, a male driver and a female front passenger both had been killed outright by the impact. It was a straight piece of road and there were no skid marks as to show that the car had attempted to slow down prior to colliding with the bridge.

The policeman on the scene knew that this was a murder of the female and suicide of the driver. It appears that it had been an ongoing domestic dispute over a period of time. He thought that this was going to happen sooner or later between these two.

Money has also an influence on what people do to other people. Take for instance a fire in Hemel Hempstead, persons trapped. On arrival efforts were being made by the Fire service to rescue a male person inside the house which was well ablaze. Talking to police on scene I asked if any body else was known to be in the house,

'No, all they had was an anonymous phone call saying house on fire, man inside.'

They went onto say, 'We do have marker on the house, saying the person may deal in drugs and can be violent.'

When the body was recovered the person had been stabbed, he didn't have any burns on him. The query at the time was whether he had died of this stab wound or smoke inhalation. It was found out much later that he was a drug dealer and some on had taken a dislike to him. He had died from the stab wound prior to the house being set on fire.

A Friday evening, calls were coming in to a large scale fight in a Mosque in Bury Park Luton. As I was arriving on scene I was amazed at the number of police that were present dealing with setting up a traffic system for police and ambulances that were still making there way to the scene.

Huge numbers of people were milling around in the street outside the mosque. The police had their dogs out trying to hold the crowd back. The first ambulance was just leaving the scene with one male with severe stab wounds. The second ambulance was dealing with another stab wound patient.

I entered the mosque to utter bedlam, people shouting, arguing and telling us to look after the injured people. The police were trying to sort out what was what. I found four other patients with knife wounds and various abrasions. I called up control and asked for another four ambulances to attend the scene, the last one had to travel from Letchworth ambulance base. So I had to stay in the mosque till the last ambulance arrived to take the last patient away.

As I patched up each patient to hand over to the crews when they arrived, the police had managed to take control of the situation. The mosque was now completely cleared apart from two remaining patients, senior police officer, police man and me.

As I handed over the last patient over the ambulance crew, I asked the Chief inspector what had gone off to course all this mayhem.

He replied, 'The fight had started over money, and it appeared at this stage that some of the taxi drivers were not given enough of their takings over to the mosque and the discussion had got out of hand'.

'Well you can say that again' I said as we shock hands and left for the hospital.

In all, we took six patients to the Luton & Dunstable hospital. One male died from his injuries, the other five patients were discharged from hospital over a period of eight days.

And when you think it cannot happen to anyone you know, we had two of our staff on St. Albans station that had relatives murdered.

Les, his sister-in-law was murdered. It appeared that there had been some kind of attack on her prior to her murder a few days earlier. Our colleague lived at the home of his wife mother's house and the sister in law had moved back to her mother's house after the break up of the marriage. One night the estranged husbands broke into the house and shot his wife dead.

He drove off and was latter found by the police, in his car on the hard shoulder of the M4 slumped over the steering wheel. They had stopped to check out why the car was stopped, as they opened the door of his car, to ask, they found that he had tried to shoot himself in the head. All he had achieved was that he had shot his eyes out. He had put the gun too far forward on his temple when he pulled the trigger of the gun to kill himself.

Hugh lost his sister to a murderer. She was on her way home one evening she got off the bus to walk the half mile home, she never arrived. There was a massive hunt for her but she was not found until a month after, seven miles from her home. It was believed that after she was murdered and her body had been stored in a freezer, for some time during the period she had been missing. This was due to the condition of her body. No one was ever charged with her murder.

And perhaps one of the up and coming reasons for murder "Terrorism"

Hertfordshire had three attacks by the IRA, two being of no consequence, but one proved fatal for the carriers, or as the police called it, "An own goal". If these attacks had managed to get to their destination this would have been murder.

I was at home about 22.00hrs. A phone call from control asked me to attend St Peters Street, St. Albans as the gas show rooms had exploded. Whilst enroute from my home in Harpenden two police cars, came up fast behind me sirens flashing headlights and I thought I was shifting. (I wasn't called balloon tyres for nothing) I thought, this looks like a good job. No progress report had come from the first ambulance yet, and I was about half a mile away when the first ambulance called up to give a Situation report (sitrep).

They reported that there had been an explosion outside the Barclays bank in St. Peters Street, one male had been blown off his pedal cycle which was about 50yds from the explosion, and there were believed to be two deceased persons at the site of the explosion.

The rendezvous point was at the rear of the Civic Centre. My crew then gave the full situation of the scene. Les who was an L/A had been with the London Ambulance Service (LAS) and had attended bombings in London, so he was an "old hand".

He told me 'They were sitting at the ambulance station in St. Albans, when they heard a bang I knew what it was straight away. The Fire service bells went and then our phone rung, it was control telling us to come here'

'One male person had been blown off his bike but he was more shocked than injured, but at the site of explosion over there.'

He pointed out to the entrance of Barclays bank.

'I think two people have been blown to pieces, one person has gone into the Bank the door having blown off and the other have person has gone out into the open area'.

Meeting up with a police Inspector it appears that an Army Band had been playing at the Civic Centre Arena, the police were in the area knowing that the band had been targeted before. The area had been cleared of people very quickly, and it appeared that no other persons were involved.

As we were talking this car came roaring down the road, we said to each other.

'What the fuck is going on here,'

A man jumps out of the car saying,

'I am In the St. Johns can I be of any help?'

Before I could say thanks, but no thanks the police inspector was not so polite and quite rightly he says to this man

'I don't know how you got in here but you had better get yourself out of here even quicker'

My director was informed and so was the Chief Officer of all this excitement! in case it went pear-shaped or there might be another device in the area, As all our training lectures, given by the police into bombings scenarios. We must consider and be aware of, the possibility of a second device.

The police then asked that all attending officers from the emergency services go to the police station, which was only a matter of yards away from this incident. The Ambulance on scene was sent back to the ambulance station. The situation for me was closed down after two hours of sitting around watching all the comings and goings of senior officers and "Other" services to the police station.

The outcome of this was explained the next day by the police to me. The police had an extra presence the area because, the Army Band had served in Northern Ireland. The two persons involved, one Female and one Male had been killed; they had been standing in the doorway of the bank acting as a courting couple when it was believed that the device had exploded prematurely killing them both instantly.

Two other a device had failed to go on railway lines. London to St Albans a device was found on the track, there had been some thought that it had been affixed to a train but had fallen off and harmlessly exploded on the track. A similar device either planted or had fallen off a moving train near Stevenage had exploded, but that was only caused minimal damage.

Animal rights group had an ambulance crew and officers, and all the other emergency service's tied up for hours, whilst the Army Bomb disposal squad went through the Royal Mail sorting office in Watford.

Early one afternoon we were called by the police to a minor explosion at the Watford Royal Mail sorting office. We along with the fire service were asked to stand bye awaiting the arrival of the Bomb disposal squad. The call had come in at 1500hrs. On the arrival of the Bomb squad they had to sort through several hundred bags of post. According to the senior police officer on scene they were looking for packages containing video tapes that had been filled with an explosive material.

The Bomb disposal arrived on scene with their mechanical robot. The police knew who had sent them and what make of package to look for. After ten hours of searching eight other packages were found, if these packages had been opened by the recipient they could at the very least have caused serious injuries or possibly killed them.

CHAPTER 4:
Suicides

The majority of suicides are a cry for help, the person has either got to some point in their life where they cannot cope with all that's going in their head, some cannot cope with someone leaving them, it is a cry for help for them to come back, or want somebody in there life to stay with them. Others who do carry out the successful suicide have either sought help but still cannot cope, or they go for it and do not think of the people who are left behind.

When I first started in the service it was quite noticeable that most of the attempted suicides were female. By the time the seventies came along the trend had turned the other way. Women power was coming and you could tell, they were more confident in the way they dressed, talked, acted and in their demeanour.

It was the young men who lost confidence, and it was them who started to take there lives. By the time I had left the service it was the young men who were committing suicide at a very high rate. This age group being the eighteen and twenty six years olds.

When I first started in the service we were based near three large mental hospitals housing a population of over three and half thousand patients, Hill End, Napsbury and Shenley. These three big hospitals are now all closed down, with the land and some of the non listed buildings sold off and large housing estates built on them.

We were called on a frequent basis to suicides and attempted suicides to these patients. Most of the successful ones, were the ones who walked into the path of trains or laying on the track or jumping off the platforms in front of people awaiting a train. This caused serious physiological problems to the people that witnessed these traumatic incidents.

RTA's being another method used. We attended a call to a lady under a bus. She was obviously deceased even though we were not allowed to say this. The bus driver was suffering from severe shock as he told us that this lady was walking along the pavement pushing a pram, then the next second she let go of the pram and ran straight into the path of his bus.

A woman was holding onto the pram, and in it, was just a plastic doll!

We then guessed that she had come out of the adjacent hospital which had a unit for mothers suffering from post natal depression. On the arrival of the police we informed them of our suspicions and we conveyed the young lady to hospital for certification.

A couple of hours later we were back at the hospital, we saw the policeman at the RTA. He confirmed that our suspicion were correct, and that her baby who was 3 months old, was safe and well in the hospital unit that the mother had walked from.

A Similar RTA a young man lying in the road next to a car with a broken leg. The elderly female driver and her equally elderly passenger were in deep shock at what had happened. It appeared that the young man had been hiding in the bushes and run out straight into their path of their car. We did all the necessary aid on him loaded him onto the ambulance and went off to hospital. Whilst enroute to the casualty department at St. Albans City hospital I asked what had happened.

He said 'I want to die and I thought this was going to be the answer to my problem.'

I replied 'All you have done is upset two elderly females, broken your leg, so you won't be up to anything for some little while. But hopefully you will get some help when you return to the hospital.'

He was not very complementary about the two ladies and said 'They should have killed me not break my fucking leg, fucking women drivers'

Well that wasn't the end to the story because about three weeks later we were called to the rear of Napsbury hospital where a railway line runs from St. Pancras London to the north. A person had been hit by a train., Whilst we were walking up the line looking for all the main parts of the body you can find so that you can take them to the hospital for certification, we came across bits of plaster of paris and then we found a large part of a leg with a plaster cast on it, yes it turned out to be our man who had run out in front of the car three weeks earlier, so unfortunately he had got his wish to die.

The help he needed? It seems as if he didn't unfortunately.

My first exposé to the other side of life so to speak, in my role of ambulance man (sheltered life and all that) was to a lesbian. It came as a shock to me that this girl had taken an overdose of pain killers all because she had had an argument with her girl friend. We conveyed her to the casualty unit at St. Albans and on arrival at the unit she said she needed to go to the toilet, she turned around to me and said.

'I am going into the Gents'

A shout from the sister on duty a quick response was.

'You are certainly not young lady'.

After she had her stomach washed out, the casualty doctor had her admitted to Hill End hospital. In those days if you did take an over dose or tried an attempt on your life you were immediately dispatched off to a mental hospital for help. On arrival we walked towards the ward she was being admitted to, she said she was not going on that fucking ward as the sister made her wear a night dress and she only wore pyjamas.

She asked us to take her to another ward! It took some persuasion to get her to go to this ward, as it's out of our hands, which ward she was allocated to, but we said we would try to persuade the sister to swap her over to the ward she wanted. Once inside the ward she got sorted out alright! We ran off pretty smartish!

Gassing was a popular method until it changed to natural gas. One lady called us to say she was sticking her head in the oven,as she had had enough of living and she wanted to die We knew this couldn't happen, as the country had just changed over from coal gas. So off we went to see this lady, on arrival we walked into the house announcing ourselves, we found the lady in the kitchen. Sure enough she had her head in the oven and she even placed a pillow to rest her head on, but we noticed the oven was an electric one!

Now my wife is never impressed being called to any incident when she is out with me in the car. On one occasion we had just picked up my 40th birthday cake from her sisters and not quite arrived back at our home, when I was called back by control to nearly the same place we had left! So there was my wife hanging on for dear life to this beautifully iced birthday cake on her lap, in a box, as we rushed off to deal with this 999 call. Luckily my wife and cake arrived safely

Another time half way to my mum's, with my wife on board, control called me up to say they had a report of a flat on fire in Berkhampstead and person reported trapped inside.

Enroute control informed me the ambulance had arrived on scene and the patient had run off, having jumped out the first floor flat window. There was smoke still issuing from the window, and according to neighbours the man lived on his own.

The crew had been directed by these people from the flats the direction in which this male had run off to. At the same time control had a report of an RTA, person knocked down by a car not far from the fire, and were dispatching another ambulance. They said I could stand down from the call but they would keep me updated.

The first ambulance that had been dispatched to the flat fire had just come across this RTA and it turned out to be the person they were looking for. The second ambulance was then stood down by control. After a few minutes I was asked if I would attend the A&E department at West Herts. hospital to meet up with crew who had dealt with these incidents.

On arrival at the hospital the crew were standing by their ambulance and they had big grins on their faces so I knew this going to be good.

It appears that their patient was a young man in his mid twenties who had boarded up his flat, moved an arm chair in the middle of the room and duly set light to the flat because he had had enough of life. When the flames reached his chair he thought shit this hurts, so he got up and jumped straight out through the window which was about a twenty five foot drop to the ground, but with some luck he had only sprained his ankle. He got up and ran off down into the high street, where he promptly got run over by a car being driven by a retained fireman enroute to the fire station to jump on the appliance to attend the flat fire! What are the chances of this happing?

We could not work the odds out on that so we gave up. The patient sustained a fractured leg, slight burns to his thighs and cuts to his wrist which he had carried out himself, and slight cuts from the window he had jumped through. He left hospital three weeks later.

As every ambulance person will tell you as soon as you switch the kettle on at the station to make a cup of tea the phone will ring from control, they seem to know what you are doing, and then they say to you, proceed to some where or other.

One early shift I was checking the ambulance for the coming days work and my crew mate has just boiled the kettle when the phone rings. I hear yes, ok yes, ok then he pulls the rope to open the garage doors. 'We have a call in Radlett'

A village three miles from our station

The road we were called to has the most expensive houses to buy in this village. The call was to a female shouting down the phone he's dead, he's dead, and control had just managed to gain enough information of the address for us to attend. So we speculated about what an earth we were going to other than this person was dead, but in our experience most cases we had been called to were not that simple.

On arrival at the house the front door was open, so we entered this very big house and we could hear this sobbing and wailing coming from one of the down stairs rooms. We gingerly pushed the door open and walked in announcing who we were, we got no response from the female, who was sitting on the sofa in the lounge my colleague sat down beside her and tried to get some information from her. I went up stairs to see what I could find, hoping I would either find, or get a call giving me a clue as to where or what I was looking for. I hunted up stairs in all the bedrooms, under the beds, in the cupboards then my colleague shouted to me

'He's down stairs in the cupboard under the stairs'.

I rushed down the stairs two at a time opened the door to this big cupboard under the stairs to be confronted by a pair legs swinging in front my eyes, I looked up and I found a male hanging with a rope around his neck, to be honest it took a second for me to take this in, I can remember how shocked I was at this. I don't know why or what I was expecting to find really, so that's why it shocked me. I went back into the room to give the thumbs up to my colleague that I had found him and that he was well and truly dead.

I went out to the ambulance to inform control over the radio what we had found, I asked for the police to attend. Going back into the house my colleague had found out that, this was the ladies husband and it was his 40th birthday that day. She had made loads of arrangements for him to celebrate his birthday, she had spent nearly an hour looking for him when she found him under the stairs. It was a very traumatic event for her because as I said it had shocked me too.

My colleague went off to phone her G.P., so he could come and perhaps help her and to certify her husband death. My colleague went to the cupboard to see for himself what the situation, even he remarked how shocked he was.

The police came and we told him what we had been told, took him to the cupboard so he could see for himself and then the G.P. turned up. As we were leaving I heard the wife shout out the "Selfish bastard".

Perhaps having loads of money is not every-thing, as a call comes into another posh village, Harpenden. To a female who had overdosed on pills. This happened in the middle of the night. We got to the road ok but this house only had a name and no number. Now these calls are always a nightmare at the best of times even during the day. You don't know which end of the road it well be, or what side of the road to start looking, and at night you cannot see the names on house very well either. They can be anywhere, on the gate, the hedge, front door or on the house. I understand that no one wants to leave their love-ones alone when they are ill, and come to look for us if they are the only person in the house. Not like the fire service when they are called normally the house is on fire, no problem, the local police know their patch very well, or if not some one normally comes out of the house to wait for them to attend.

The male relative told our control he would leave the porch light on and a bedroom light on as well so we could easily find the house. We turned into the road which was quite long. Not knowing which side of the road this house was on and you would be surprised at that time in the night how many houses have porch lights and bedroom lights on! Our torches were of little use, I got out on my side of the road to look at the house names, by which time a further call had been made to control, asking them

'Where the fucking hell was the ambulance I called for hours ago'

Which of course was not true, we had arrived in the road six minutes after the call. Control informed him of our position in the road so he came out of his house shouting his head off at us.

Having ascertained that she taken an overdose of some prescription medicine we removed the lady from the bedroom and conveyed her to the casualty department at St. Albans. We passed the patient over to the sister in charge and warned her that the ladies husband was an obnoxious shit. She could have a problem with him as he had been shouting at us about how long we had taken to get to the house and calling us a bunch of amateurs. I bit my tongue as I was the junior part of the crew, my colleague being one of the old boys; he just calmly let it go over his head.

We walked out of the department as the husband walked up to my colleague and said 'I better not see any of this in the papers tomorrow because I can assure you, your feet wont touch the ground'.

I walked towards him to confront him my colleague trod on my foot to stop me, he replied 'Of course not sir'

I could have punched my colleague for not telling him to go forth and multiply. and to tell him we are a professional service not some tin pot army.

He replied' Don't worry son his time is coming'.

This incident and others, of a similar problem of lighting led us to getting better lighting on our vehicles.

Some incident can tie up resources for sometime as one evening turned into a marathon. A man had decided to jump off a moving train between Berkhampstead and Tring railway stations. It appeared that a male was sitting in the carriage of a train bound for Manchester when he suddenly got up, forced the door open in his carriage as it was still travelling quite fast and jumped out of the door! The shocked passengers in the carriage pulled the emergency cord, and as you can imagine these trains don't stop on a sixpence they can take up to three miles to stop. This being a very rural area there are no lights as on a main road. So it was a case of ambulance, police and railway staff to starting to walk from Berkhampstead towards Tring. The police had also sent some policemen from the Tring direction. The man was eventually found by the police in a very serious condition.

With excellent support from railway staff they commandeered a train to take our equipment and crew to the location of the man. Another train was sent from the opposite direction so that we could load the patient onto that train and bring him back into Berkhampstead rail station. Where the ambulance was parked, he was then conveyed to hospital.

Whilst not every call appears to be what it seems. We are called to person hit by a train between St. Albans and Harpenden. Parking up on a bridge near to where the body was reported hit, in the distance we saw what looked like a body lying by the railway track. Off we march down the track which is not as easy as it sounds. The ground is uneven, large pieces of gravel and as for walking on the sleepers give up as they are not a pace apart. We did check before our enforced hike that all trains had been stopped. As we got nearer to the body we said to each other that's good at least it looks like its all in one bit!

We got along side this man, we saw he was dressed in a uniform of a railway worker! Better still he was still breathing so as we bent down to touch him, and we asked him 'Are you ok mate'

He jumped up in shock.

'What the fuck are you doing here?'

We told him that we had been called to a person knocked down by a train at this location. After a bit of banter between us, it transpires that as it was a nice day he had just lain down and gone off to sleep! As you do at work. We told him that we had been called by the police, he was very agitated at this, because just a few hundred yards behind us, were the police. We met them and told them what was going on and they said.

'Really will sort him out'

Oh dear the cost of a nap on a nice day!

Situations, are they caused by watching Television? I wondered this after attending to a lady who had set light to herself. It was strange because at the time, Buddhist monks were doing a similar thing. It was in the newspapers on TV news, perhaps the person got the idea from these reports. The call was to a tiny Hamlet called Gustard Wood it was well after midnight.

On arrival we were sent to the back of this very large house by a man (I never did find out what the relationship was) to a person sitting in the middle of the lawn with severe burns and still smouldering. If we hadn't been told the patient was female we would never had known, because of the severity of the burns mostly second and third degree burns to over 70% of her body We got a sheet from a bed in the house and soaked it in water and then wrapped the woman in the sheet to place her on the stretcher, as we did so we nearly dropped her because of the intense heat still coming from her body.

We rushed her into St. Albans casualty unit because we were not allowed to convey straight into the burns unit, which in our case would have been Mount Vernon. There was no kind of treatment we could give her, apart from hold the oxygen mask tube to her mouth, no pain killing gas or cooling jell or burns sheets. After several hours of waiting while the doctors tried to get fluid into her, dress her wounds they contacted Mount Vernon hospital to see if she could be sent there.

Whilst we were waiting for this transfer to happen my colleague and I talked the job through with each other. We both had noticed a For Sale board outside the house but the strange thing about it was, it was being sold by a government department. We also over heard the man who had followed us by car into the hospital talking to some one on the phone, a very well known person as well. It appeared that this persons? Had been involved in a high profile crime, which had been on TV and newspapers. Perhaps that's why the house was up for sale by a government department. After being treated at St. Albans we then conveyed her to the burns unit at Mount Vernon, We heard a few days latter that the lady died from her burns.

As I said at the beginning of this chapter as young men took over from the young women for committing suicides. Theirs was more masculine in the way they chose to die. Taken a shot gun to the heads, this is very messy, and I am glad when I can just say to the police 'It's over to you'.

To hang themselves from trees, one of these young men had got up in the middle of the night and hung himself in the back garden of his parent's house. The trauma he caused by this act on his parents, he would never know. It's something that a parent never contemplates or hopes it will never happen, the death of their child. To die before their parent in these circumstances is even more traumatic. To find your child dead, hanging in your garden, will cause untold stress and anguish to his parents. The other was another young male, it was near to Christmas time in an open area in Dunstable. He had managed to climb a tree with some rope he found from somewhere, several of his mates had found him and tried to rescue him but they were unable to get him down from the tree before he died.

Even more gruesome was a patient from Napsbury hospital, he had walked into London Colney High Street from where the hospital was situated. He waited in a bus queue but didn't get on the bus, but as soon as it moved off he went and put his head under the rear wheels of the bus just as it moved off.

Once I spent over an hour talking to a man who had climbed onto a roof of a hotel, he had fallen out with his boy friend and he wouldn't come down until he saw him again. Unbeknown to me his boyfriend had left the hotel and had gone back home to Brighton, and we had no way of contacting him. I climb up a ladder next to him on the roof to ask him about what was concerning him. No matter what I said I got no response. I talked to him about any thing I could think of football, government, weather, what kind of relationship he had with his boyfriend was he concerned about HIV or any other illnesses, anything I could talk about.

But no matter how I tried to engage him into conversation on any topic, just to get him to talk, he just refused to engage in any form of conversation with me. After an hour and half, he got on the ladder with me and came down was it because the alcohol had worn off, or it might have been because I was boring him so much, as I can normally talk for hours. And that can be confirmed by all my staff who say I can talk for hours about fuck all! The police met us on the ground, which promptly handcuffed and arrested him for being drunk and disorderly.

CHAPTER 5:
Robberies

We are constantly told every decade by Hertfordshire police, that our great county is the safest county in the country for violent crime and murders. So like murders I haven't been to many.

A bank raid in Hemel Hempstead, now this was something different, I thought, I had never been to one of these before. It was off our patch so it took us about 10 minutes to get there. My colleague and I were thinking about any money lying about on the floor if the robbers had dropped some as they made off, could we fill our pockets, just joking about it really because as we knew we wouldn't do it.

On arrival the world and his aunt were there, the local press, police by the hundreds and most of the surrounding householders. The first thing we did, was to put our caps on, the last thing we wanted was another bollocking from our station officer for being in the press not properly dressed, as we were always being told off for not wearing our caps.

We gathered from the senior police officer on scene that there was a male who was a bank employee with facial injuries, who was inside the bank and we could only go into the bank through the window next to the door. Having ascertained that the patient who was the manager of the bank had been hit in the face and knocked out, I went back to the ambulance to get our carry chair, I asked the police officer in charge to open the door as we couldn't carry the manager out through the window. I heard some police person say 'Well that's fucked up any evidence'

'Sorry I'll leave the patient inside if you like until you open the door'

The door was opened very reluctantly.

I still got my got my bollocking thanks to the press, as I had removed my cap, but my mate managed to keep his on, creep! Because later that night, there were pictures of us carrying the patient out of the bank on the front page of the evening local paper.

They say it's a small world having been called to an RTA. On arrival there were two cars across the road but not badly damaged? This road in St. Albans is only a minor one with hardly any traffic around. Two men were out of the car, and two men still in the back of one of the cars. As I approached them I knew the two men standing outside the car and as I looked into the car I recognized the other two men as well. One of them was my old boss at the Salvation Army printing works.

They had been rammed by one of the cars and robbed of the entire wages for the whole of the printing works. They were quite shaken up and my former boss and his colleagues had been thumped, not badly, but enough to need hospital attention. We were waiting for the police to arrive, so that we could inform them of the situation.

Up turns one policeman quite oblivious to what had really happened here, just like us thinking that it was just an ordinary RTA, but once we told him, he turned green and all hell was let loose. Don't move from here don't do this don't do that (Don't Panic) We said sorry but the two patients would be at the hospital and you can send someone there to talk to them. That went down like a lead balloon so before he had another fit, we took off. On route to hospital it was strange talking to my old boss and former colleagues about things and what a small world it was to meet up this way.

I was at a meeting and got paged by our control informing me that a shooting had taken place involving the police, and that one of my officers was enroute to the scene. They would keep me updated if it turned out to be more serious than the information they currently had. After the meeting had finished, I got in touch with my officer who had attended the shooting to find out what had happened.

It turned out that the police had been tipped off that an armed raid was to take place at a gun shop in Park Street near St. Albans. The police were waiting inside the shop and outside as well, waiting for the bad guys to turn up and raid the shop!

Now I must say it is unusual for the police not to have one of our units standing by in the area in case it all went pair shaped, like this appeared to have done, but they didn't in this case for what ever reason.

In walked three guys armed with sawn off shot guns to be confronted by armed police. The police in their usual politically correct manner asked them to put their guns down. They declined, and shots were fired by these men and the police. One of the robbers was hit three times but he just kept on walking towards the policeman who was doing the shooting at him and eventually he went down. The policeman who shot him approached him, and told my colleague he was so shocked at him still walking towards him that he asked him while he was lying on the ground putting bandages on him if he was on drugs. A feeble response came back 'No'

To which the police man replied 'I bet you wish you were now.'

I thought this was brilliant remark worthy of any Clint Eastwood film.

The men were taken to hospital and the most serious one stayed in the hospital for a week or two, you couldn't go any where in the hospital without being confronted by armed policemen during those weeks.

All these young men were under 21 years of age and had already served time in prison for other serious offences and apparently were quite notorious, but all had been released early from prison!

I was called out one night being the nearest to a male beaten up in a side street and no back up from an ambulance for at least 20minutes

On arrival I found a male unconscious with head wounds, not that serious I thought, so I tried to get a response with all my usual pain inducing methods, to see what his level of coconscious.

I decided he was deeply unconscious and put him on oxygen, placed an airway into him, still no reflex of any kind. Then I noticed two small brown bars lying on the ground next to him which I wasn't certain what they were, I picked them up and found to my surprise that they were cannabis resin bars. The police had just arrived and I handed them over to them, and gave them a sitrep of the condition of the patient, which I thought at the time was serious. They asked my permission to check his pockets to find out who he was, in case this job was going to be treated as attempted murder so that they could get some identity, and inform his relatives!

Whilst going through his pockets they found even more of these bars of cannabis by which time the police were coming in droves, and closing off the roads. In the mean time I am still waiting for the ambulance to arrive. The police were thinking that this person was a dealer and things had gone badly wrong for him in some way. The ambulance arrived and the crew agreed with me that he was deeply unconscious. But, like me, they thought it funny because it appeared to be a minor injury to his head. We wondered if it could be that he had taken any drugs, to be in this unconscious condition. He was transported to hospital escorted by two police officers..

The next morning I was having a meeting with the A&E consultant, and asked how the male person that I had attended the night previously was.

'Oh him, he got up within 10 minutes of arriving here, he didn't want to stay or be examined by us, and so he was taken off by the police for tea and biscuits'

I don't think.

I knew something was not quite right about this person but I must admit he was a good actor or he didn't feel any pain, or had a gagging reflex to being able to tolerate an airway down his throat.

The police caught up with me a day after this call to write a statement about the drugs I had found, I asked 'Was on drugs, because of the way he had fooled me'.

'No, we had our own doctor check him as well. But he was very well known to the Metropolitan police for shamming his demise'

You can say that again.

Car jacking is the up coming way of stealing cars. As car manufactures make it more difficult for the little morons to steal them. So they have to have the keys. One way is waiting at petrol stations and waits for an idiot driver to leave his keys in the car and go off to pay, as one driver found to his cost in Dunstable.

We were alerted to a man last seen being driven off on the bonnet of a car at high speed, being chased by the police! Bob the station officer attended the incident and came back to station to tell about.

It appears that the injured person had been filling his car up with fuel and had left his keys in the ignition, when two young men jumped into the car and drove off. The owner instinctively jumped on the bonnet of his car. He was driven out of the store, around a roundabout, through two sets of pedestrian lights, one major set of traffic lights, over two cross roads and two further roundabouts. All this time clinging to bonnet for his life, he was finally thrown off the bonnet, on an industrial estate in the middle of a dual carriageway. The whole distance was just over two miles, he was seriously injured and taken to Luton & Dunstable hospital. The two thieves never stopped, they just kept going after the owner had been thrown off. They were caught later, by the police.

CHAPTER 6:
Even off duty

Even off duty I had this knack of coming across incidents, mostly RTA s, or the odd drunk or person collapsed.

While on holiday in some little village in Wales I came across a male lying in the middle of the road. I stopped and parked across the road so that the patient and I would be protected against any cars using the road, thinking really I stood more of a chance of being run over by a flock of sheep. As I got down on my knees I could see he was having an epileptic fit, so I just stayed with him to insure his airway was ok and that he didn't thrash around too much to injury himself.

Then several women came up to me, and I told them I was an ambulance man and did they know this man, and does he suffer from fits but no one answered. Then more women appeared and I asked if some one would call an ambulance, still no reply and I felt as if I was being slowly pushed to one side by these women. When a man appeared and said to me 'I would get back into your car mate if I was you'

I told him what I was,

He replied 'If you care for your own safety you had better go'

I was completely shocked at this, I must admit the women were getting hostile towards me even though they never spoke to me. I got back into my car and my wife Val said to me, 'Why are you not staying with the patient"

I told her what had been said to me, she couldn't believe it. We have never been back to Wales again

We now go to Scotland for holidays which we love. But once again, driving along looking at the scenery, once again in the middle of nowhere, when two motor bikes whizzed passed us as though I was going backwards. I wondered how long they would last on roads racing along like that.

Yes, you guessed, not long after wards even though we diverted through this little village, we came out the other end and there was a motor cyclist laying in the road. His mate who was on the other bike had parked at the side of the road. So I jumped out of my car got my first aid bag, told the people around who I was. I spoke to the cyclist who was fully conscious as I checked him over. I recognised his leathers and helmet as one of the motor cyclists who had whizzed past me a few miles up the road.

He said he had been confronted by a car turning right into the village and he had clipped the car trying to avoid it, he was suffering from a fracture of the tibia and fibula. He was lucky because of the speed he was going past me it could have been much more serious. Some one told me they had called an ambulance so that was fine. I reassured him he would be ok, and with that a man came through the thong of onlookers saying 'Stand back I am an ambulance man"

'Oh good' I said 'That's two us, we can do a bit of traction and put some triangular bandages around his leg.'

But before we started that, another voice from the crowd called 'Stand back I am an ambulance man.'

Crikey I thought three ambulance men in the middle of nowhere what ever next. Yes another one turns up so I said 'Well that's four of us'

So he said 'Well is there anything I can do'

I said 'Yes please can you get a pen and paper'

He said 'Sure is that all, do you want it, so that you can write a report?'

"No", I said,

'It's so you can draw an ambulance that's the only thing that's missing'

Everybody started laughing, the ambulance arrived, and we all assisted the crew to load the patient into the ambulance, and as the driver shut the door

'I said 'With all these ambulance staff around here we ought to have a union meeting'.

He came back with a quick response and in his quiet Scottish accent said

'No there's too many of us'!

Brilliant I thought he was right. Off they went, to the nearest hospital some 50 odd miles away. People in the south east of England don't appreciate how near they are to a hospital in case of trouble.

Going home one dark and wet evening I was driving on the M1 motorway between junctions 9 and 8 with my two children, when I came across an RTA, it was a mini van that had collided with the central crash barrier and another car.

No mobile phones in those days so I hoped that some one had called an ambulance from one of the road side phone boxes. Having made sure that I was parked in a safe position, I told my children to stay in the car. Reaching the van I noticed nobody was around, even though several cars were at the scene! I soon found out why. I approached the first person, to find he had been decapitated, on checking it was a male. The other person still in the van was also a male he was also deceased.

The police were quickly on the scene and as they came over to me I quickly told them who I was, and what the situation was regarding the patients. They were pleased I was there so they didn't have deal with the patients. They asked if would stay with them until the ambulance arrived. The police then proceeded to get the scene sealed off and the traffic problems sorted out.

As the ambulance arrived I noticed it was one from my station at St. Albans, so I knew the crew straight away which certainly helped in dealing with the situation. The crew members were an old boy, a Leading ambulance man, (L/a) and a fairly new member of staff. The L/a., moans about almost anything and was no exception on this occasion either, said 'I was just going to have my dinner before we got this call now I've got to deal with this, it aint right and what are doing here Ennis?'

(One of many names I was called) 'Just came across it' I said,

'A likely story'

The poor new bod just shrugged his shoulders as if to say, well you know him better than me. I got the new member of staff to help me while the L/a fluffed about, we got on with dealing with the patients getting them to the stretchers, we didn't have body bags in those days, and wrapped the patients in blankets, the whilst L/a was still going on in his usual manner.

The new member of staff said 'I'm glad you're here Enners, I don't think I could have coped, with him'!

I took this as a complement. I knew what he was trying to say, this L/a took a bit of getting used to.

Funny thing not long after this incident, I was going up to London with my daughter and we had just got onto the M1 at junction 6, I thought there was not much traffic around when this car overtook me going at some lick. He was in lane 3 and I saw him suddenly twitch as he caught his rear wheel between the edge of the tarmac and the central reservation. He failed to control his car and it started to spin, I knew he was going to crash, he did, straight into a bridge support. It was a severe impact, I parked up, got my daughter out of the car and up the embankment out of the way.

I approached the car and as I opened the door I could see he had been killed out right by the impact. Some one else stopped and I sent him off to the phone box to call for an ambulance and the police. The crew, who turned up, were from Garston Ambulance station, a crew that I hadn't seen much of, but a least we recognised each other. Once the police turned up, it was the same police crew I had met at the other fatal RTA. I proceeded to inform them what had happened here I said 'this one is also deceased'.

He said this was the second fatal RTA in a mile and a half; the other units are dealing with that's why the traffic is so light. He said to me

'I think we ought to have you banned from using this road you are nothing but bloody trouble.'

I had to attend coroner's court for this accident as I had witnessed it. I found out from the police that the driver was attached to a Middle Eastern Embassy in London. He was also a Prince in his own country. I wished then, that I had submitted the bill for having my suit cleaned from all the blood I got on it.

Another very serious accident I came across was on the North Circular just up from Staples Corner London, I was with my first wife and going home after having been shopping at Ikea, On the opposite carriageway I saw two children lying in the road and just one person looking down on them. As I couldn't stop on the opposite carriageway, I went down to Staples Corner to come back to these children, I was in my own car which I had a magnetic blue light and two tone horns and got to the scene fairly quickly. There was still only one person present, who, I believe said that he was the car driver who had collided with these two children.

These boys were aged between 6years and 9 years old. Both were unconscious, both had serious head and leg injuries. An Ambulance had been called but had not arrived, neither had the police. I managed to put an airway into both of them and insured they kept breathing. There was not much else I could do without assistance from medical help.

The police arrived on the scene first and came up to me and said 'What's the situation doc'

I said 'it's very serious and it's likely to prove' (which is the term we used if we thought it could be fatal)

'Oh shit so are you ok to stay until the ambulance arrives? Whilst we close off the road and gets some help here.'

'No problem' I said

'But before you rush off I am an ambulance man not a doctor'

'That's better still'

He said as he rushed off. It always seems a long time waiting for an ambulance even though it wasn't really that long. As LAS crew arrive on scene I was so pleased to see them. They came over to me and said 'What do you want us to do Doc.'

I told them I was an ambulance officer with Hertfordshire.

'Thank god for that we hate doctors getting involved, we thought it was strange that a doctor would have stopped at an accident as they don't usually'.

'True' I said.

We quickly but with great care loaded both these children in to the same ambulance I offered to go with them, to look after one of the children whilst the other crew member looked after the other child. They replied it was fine as they were only 5 minutes away from Park Royal hospital and would "Blue light" them in and have a medical team standing by.

It may seem strange to readers now that this happened, but in the "Old Days" ambulances had two stretchers and it was the norm to carry two or more patients at one time, but thankfully times have moved on. Realistically you can only look after one patient at a time unless the patients have minor injuries.

I rang the police up the following day and spoke to a Police Inspector who had recognised my name from the report of the accident to ask how the two children were. 'Unfortunately' even with the all best efforts by every body they both died'

Whilst it was no a surprise to me, I was still very sadden by the news.

There are always a funny stories to RTAs I witnessed. I was following a bubble car in Watford High Street when the car suddenly accelerated through a set of traffic lights that were changing from green to red, as it took a left turn it rolled over onto its side. A policeman had been standing on the corner, saw the whole thing happen in front of him. We pulled the door open together, and out crawled this man on his hands and knees. As he stood up in a drunken state with a cigarette in his mouth still alight! But it had bent in two; he was unaware of it, because he was still sucking away on it. It was so comical, and I started to laugh but the policeman was trying not to. The man was not injured he was too drunk and relaxed. He just rocked backwards and forwards whilst the policeman tried to talk to him. He was arrested and taken off by the police still drawing on his bent cigarette.

Driving on the M5 to Cornwall, to pick up my wife, Val, she had been on holiday. I was driving through sleet, snow, and rain for about three miles, the maximum speed realistically for any one, was around 20 mph. I noticed on the northbound carriageway four cars all over the place it looked serious so I stopped. I got my gear out of the car and went across to the opposite carriageway. Now I have been on RTAs on the M1, M25 and the A1M, when it would be impossible to do this, also I would not even attempt to do it either. I couldn't get over how little traffic there was on this road in January. I went to the most damaged car first, where there was one male with head and back injuries and in another car two patients male and female with only minor injuries. Some one said that they had called the emergency services, sure enough up turn three fire appliances first! Four police cars and about ten minutes after all this, one ambulance. Ah well I thought nothing changes everybody has more resources than the ambulance service.

When every body had been sorted out, and the second ambulance turned up to convey the minor injury patients to hospital, it left me to get back to my car. The police were quite concerned how I was going to get back across the carriageway to my car. To be honest I was not sure if they were joking but I don't suppose they were. I had already informed who I was, and where I had come from and if this accident had happened in my area there would be a ten mile queue in each direction by now. I am not kidding there was not a queue anywhere ,if there was one car every twenty seconds passing on the carriageway where my car was parked, I think I might be exaggerating, but I got escorted back to my car by two women police officers!

A little out of the ordinary on a Sunday afternoon, I walked down into my village in Redbourn to post a letter. This only being 100yds away from my house, I saw this little girl walking down the High Street. It was pouring of rain, she only had a little jumper and skirt on, there was a man about 5yds away from her, looking in a shop window, being a nosey bugger I said ,'Is the little girl with you?'

"No' he said

'She's been walking up and down for a couple of minutes I don't think she is with anybody'

So I went up to her and I said 'Is your mummy and daddy here?'

(I guessed she was about three years of age)

All she said was 'No'

I thought I cant leave her here so I said 'Lets go home and find mummy and daddy,' She held my hand and off we went back to my house. My wife was surprised wife when I walked back into the house. I go and post a letter, come back with a little girl, 'What a good exchange rate' I said.

Being so young she didn't know were she lived but we had her Christian name but no surname, so we called the police. A policeman turned up, to see what, when and how. He said they had had no reports of any missing children within the village, but he would tour around to see if he could find any body walking around. It was raining so he said it would be likely that the parents would be the only ones out this afternoon, so off he went. He came back in about half an hour with no luck and still he had no reports, of a missing child.

I picked this child up at about 1500 hrs and it was now just after 1600hrs, if this had been either of my two children missing all this time. I know I would have missed them, because it would have been too quiet in the house. The policeman was now weighing up his options of what do next. Call Social Services, get a WPC to attend, call for more help, to start banging on doors. The only comfort he got was at lest I was an ambulance person so he wasn't worried that the child was in the wrong hands! Plus we were foster parents for the Hertfordshire County Council. My wife had changed the little girls clothes and dried her off and she was quite happy playing with our two children. At just after 1700hrs the policeman returns back to our house with the mother and farther of the little girl.

They were obviously pleased to see her safe and well, but the little girl was not fussed at all, typical I thought kids don't realise all the problems they cause us parents. Anyway they said thank you! They all went off together we never even got the clothes we put on the little girl, back either. Very Strange my wife and I thought.

I still come across incidents even though I have semi retired, I work for a private ambulance company and so far have dealt with three RTA,s one of which we had to convey a motor cyclist to hospital because the LAS, could not get an ambulance to us for at least forty minutes!.

We also witnessed a serious assault, having just left a Boxing Match! having been held in a very posh hotel in the centre of London. We saw a man flying through the air having been thrown off a flight of steps from a pub by a doorman. He landed on the pavement on his head. He was an American guy, his pals all American were well and truly drunk, and trying to interfere with us, as we attempted to put an oxygen mask, neck collar and to try and stem the bleeding from the head wound.

They kept shouting at us 'We are Fire Chiefs and paramedics back home let us take over.'

But they were so drunk they kept running off to gods knows where. Then come back and start on at us all over again. Then they wanted to sort out the door man who had thrown them and his mate out of the pub, but luckily by now the police turned up in droves. As any ambulance person will tell you that's all in a nights work now, putting up with the drunken mates of the injured person. The police and all the A&E department staff have the same problems as well. The police then have to try and sort out who has done what, and to whom and if necessary have to arrest some one. The patient was conveyed to hospital by the LAS in a very serious condition. I didn't envy the police trying to sort this one out, as we left the scene there was still a lot of shouting and pushing still going on.

CHAPTER 7:
A laugh every day

I count myself extremely lucky that in my entire service career I had the great fortune to work with a great bunch of conscientious and hard working men and women. I was lucky enough to proceed up the ladder stage by stage to become Assistant Director of Operations. The officers that worked with me, my Director, Chief Officers were all extremely loyal and helped me with advice to enable me to carry out my duties. Without this, my job would have been quite difficult to get things done. Whilst some days in the service it had its downs, with the tragedy that we all came across and dealt with. I still had great fun on the way nearly every day. For me I never woke up in the morning and thought I don't want to go to work today.

When I first started off in the service, the majority of staff were men who were twice my age. They had either served in world war two, or had done National Service, so saluting, or taking orders just came naturally to them.

I have already mentioned earlier about an "Old Boy L/a", two experiences I had with him. First whilst sitting in our control room looking out the window one Sunday afternoon, (I have a habit of taking my glasses off and putting them on the desk) the L/a., decided, for some unknown reason to pick my glasses up and would swing them back wards and forwards on the arm. Bang! As he bangs them into the desk and breaks the frame, 'Oh you had better have them back'

He says to me, and with that he gets up and walks out of the control room! No mention then or later about I will pay for them.

The second laugh was when my son Andrew was born the L/a said I could have a high chair and a play frame that had been lying around in his house for some time; he said I could have them, so I said thanks. I went to his house to pick them up after I placed them in the car and about to drive off he said '"That's a fiver you owe me!'

Another "Old boy" I was working with on an RTA, a lorry driver was trapped in his cab and the fire brigade were trying to rescue him. My crew mate, was holding the big chrome light, that comes off the fire appliance to illuminate the cab area, to assist the firemen in the cab, whilst trying to free the driver. Lighting in those days was extremely poor and this was on an unlit road, drizzling with rain, and so any kind of light was essential. When up turns the fire brigades Divisional officer, and as he walks past my mate with the light he says 'good evening Jones'

With that Jones promptly drops the light and salutes him and said 'Sir'

The light having been dropped is now completely broken, and you can imagine the scene, no light, shouting and abuse coming from the fireman inside the lorry cab in a non complementary manner. The police and I stumbled back to our vehicles to get some torches. It was impossible to manoeuvre our vehicles into a position to illuminate the scene because the lorry had gone off the road into a field. Having got as many torches as we could muster, we got back to the lorry, to help out but they were as much use as a Toc H lamp! Eventually a further fire appliance arrived on scene with another lamp, so the rescue could continue. It was a successful outcome, but my colleague was never ever allowed to forget that incident.

One of my mates who was about the same age as me, we were always in trouble for not wearing our caps, either from the station officer or the Area Superintendent; they would catch us, when they were driving around in their cars. Staff cars in those days were not marked up like today's cars. We would be called back to the station and would get a dressing down. So we came up with an idea, we screwed our hats above our heads onto the bulkhead! This was fine on the Bedford J but not on any other vehicle, but we didn't get caught as often after that.

A crew from a neighbouring station was driving along minding their own business when a car careered across the road at them head-on, forcing them to stop before colliding with them! They jumped out of the ambulance to have a go at the driver and to call the police, as they approached the car, out got this ambulance officer who was unknown to them. It turned out to be their new Area Superintendent, who had just started that day! Well a few choice words were said. He said he had stopped them because they were not wearing their caps.

Well even more choice words were exchanged, and the crew demanded an apology from him, or they would go to the Chief

Officer and have him disciplined, for his stupid behaviour in nearly having a collision with them. Being a complete arrogant twit of an officer he didn't apologise, so the crew stuck to their word and reported him to the Chief Officer. He had to apologise then, he didn't stay in charge of that area long, and left our service quite quickly after that.

I was driving a sitting car up to London and getting low on fuel, so I went into a London ambulance station situated in the east end of London. I had heard that it had a reputation for being an unruly and a militant station, but needs want and all that, so in I went and found a L/a. I asked if the station officer was around

His reply 'I run this Station if you want anything ask me'

Ok I thought 'I need fuel please!'

Just like Oliver Twist asking for more out of the book by Dickens

'Are you in a Union'

'Yes' I replied,

'I am also a shop steward'

'Which one'

'N.U.P.E'

'That's ok you can have it' he replied

'Never come onto this station and ask for a station officer again son, he books on duty here and we only see him again when he signs off duty, I and the other L/A run this station'.

'Sounds good to me' I replied.

When I got back to my station and told them where I had been they said

'Crikey you are lucky the last person we knew who went there had sugar poured into his petrol tank'

As I grew older into my thirties now, and a L/a myself, I had to train the new boys. One of them Bruce was about seven years younger than me. We were called to a large printing works with its own medical centre, and on our arrival we found an elderly man who was recovering from a fit. He was being looked after very well by the nurse on duty, as she handed the patient over to us to convey to hospital she noticed my colleague's medal ribbon on his tunic. My colleague had been in the army and served in Northern Ireland. Oh she said 'How did you get your medal'

I quickly quipped in and said 'He's very modest about it he doesn't like talking about it but he was fatally wounded'

'No' in a shocked voice

I went onto say 'Yes Twice in fact'

With that my colleague and I wheeled the patient to the ambulance trying to keep a straight face, with the Nurse in close attendance we walked through the factory, some good one minute walk. We were just about to load the patient into the ambulance when this

Nurse gave out an almighty scream and she pushed me to the floor all at the same time. 'You bastard' she shouted

'I've just realised what you have just said'

We all creased up laughing, and she enjoyed the joke, in the end.

The same colleague and I were at an RTA, when again I had to keep a straight face. On arrival a car had gone up an embankment, I jumped out of the ambulance and went to the passenger side of the car that was more damaged knowing my colleague would go to the driver's side. As I was looking after the passenger I noticed the driver of the car had turned sideways and was watching what I was doing to his friend, I noticed that the driver had long flowing blonde hair and as Bruce open the door he said 'Hello dear could you turn around'

The driver turned around saying 'I am a mate not a dear'

I knew it was a man, but I could understand why Bruce had made the mistake. I had a laugh at his expense for a little while after that.

Attending to an assault in Borehamwood, we picked up a male with slight cuts and abrasions, so we put him on the stretcher and off we went. As Bruce drove around a roundabout enroute to Barnet Hospital it caught me unawares, I lost my balance as I was standing up cleaning the patients wounds, I hit my head on something. I came round a few seconds later, to find the patient and Bruce putting me on the Stretcher! So I went to hospital on the stretcher with the patient sat opposite me, I had to be treated at Barnet hospital with some butterflies strips placed over the cut on the bridge of my nose.

Bruce said it was funny because all he heard as was driving the patient shouting.

'You had better stop mate you've done your mate in!'

That was another laugh we had all they way back to the station. We never told any one as it would have meant more paper work for us both, plus another bollocking.

The fire brigade often held social events of some description on the St.Albans Fire & Ambulance station. On one of these occasions we were sent to an RTA on the M1. My crew mate and I jumped into the ambulance and off we went out of the station onto the main road when all of a sudden we heard shouting coming from the back of our ambulance. We screeched to a halt, thinking what the hell is going on in the back of our ambulance, we ran around to the back of the ambulance, we opened the rear doors, and there was a fireman and a female sitting case driver, in a state of undress!

At first they thought we were mucking about, thinking we knew they were in the back of the ambulance, and having a laugh at their expense. Then suddenly they realised that we were not mucking about but we were going on a proper job. The fireman who was on duty, had to run back to the station in case he was missed. The next time we met up with those two members of staff we just gave them a knowing smile.

Starting our 1500hrs to 2300hrs shift one day our station officer told us to take the ambulance we were on, over to brigade workshops at Hatfield and swap over to another one. We thought it was going over there to be serviced and the other one had been serviced. This is a job we didn't like doing as it entails taking every bit of equipment off one ambulance and then putting it onto the other one. On our arrival we reported to the Chief brigade engineer.

'Right follow me'

Off we went, I was looking at my colleague thinking this is unusual. Now you got to understand the strange working of these brigade workshops. They were run by the fire service that carried out all the major overhauls of fire and ambulance vehicles and repaired damaged vehicles. The officers must have worked in the secret service during the war because they never gave you a straight answer to any questions, if you saw a new ambulance you would ask, 'Who's having that'

Or, if you saw a damaged vehicle 'What happened there?'

You always got the same answer Nothing, Not a Word! So we followed him over to the other ambulance.

"Right, now I am going to show you something 'BUT' you must not use it until a Brigade order has been issued, do I make my self clear?'

My colleague and I looked at each other and knew what each of us was thinking, what an earth is this old git going on about? He pointed to a switch on the dashboard which was new. 'This switch is connected to a set of two tone horns under the bonnet, you are the first station to have them fitted, and once again I must stress to you, you are not to use them under any circumstances until the order is issued, do I make my self clear?'

We just nodded a reply back to him

'The only reason you are the first station to have them fitted, is because you are the union shop steward' (pointing at me) 'Who has been complaining at every JSCC' (Joint Service Consultative Committee) 'meeting about the bells and how inadequate the bells are'

Now not knowing if this was a complement which I doubted very much, I think he was more concerned at the cost involved. I said in reply 'Well you ought to come out with us one day and find out for yourself the problem of the bells'.

He waved his hand at me to dismiss what I had just said. We changed over all the equipment onto this ambulance and my mate said 'If he thinks I am not going to try these out before the appointed day he is mistaken big time'

We rushed back towards our base, to get onto a quite stretch of road to try these horns out, the noise was deafening. Wow! We thought these are going to be great.

We heard the other 1500hr., crew going into St. Albans casualty unit so we thought we would share our new toy with them. We pulled up behind them at the casualty unit. But my mate thought of an idea, he called them over to our ambulance and said '"Come and listen to our engine does it seem right to you'

He opened up the bonnet, and as they peered in the engine area he got into the cab to appear to start the engine up but turned the horns on! Well one of them hit his head on the bonnet catch cutting his head open and the other one just swore at us. It was a bloody good laugh, really great. But as my mate tried to switch off the horns, they kept on going! We tried putting pillow slips into the trumpets to deaden the sound, but everyone was coming out of the casualty unit to see what an earth the noise was, and what was going on. In the end my mate said 'I'll have to own up and call the engineers out'

Well you can imagine the furore that followed. The station officer gave us a right old bollocking over it. Subsequently all fuses for the horns were removed until the appointed day on every ambulance. The poor ambulance man who hit his head on the catch had to have stitches in his wound which also went down like a horse shit sandwich. Our station officer had to fill in accident form explaining what had happened to injured ambulance mans head

There are always strange people knocking about seeking medical attention, wasting everybody's time. One bright and early with a severe frost on the ground we were called to outside a village police station in London Colney a male collapse. On arrival a male person was lying on the pavement saying he was having a heart attack!

'More like frost bite' my mate said.

We placed him into the ambulance and set off for the casualty department. Enroute I was trying to ascertain the extent of this mans illness; he was going into unconsciousness one minute, waking up the next and then looking out of one eye at me. I said to him 'Do you come from one of the mental hospitals'

This was because the hospital, was only three quarters of a mile away. With that he jumped up and started to attack me. I called my driver to call the police to meet us at the hospital. I was bigger and younger than the patient so I soon overpowered him. He was still struggling with me all the way into the hospital. On arrival at casualty the police were waiting for us, as they opened the doors to the ambulance, the patient and I fell out struggling with each other. The police took over from me and took him away. He was shouting at me and told me in no uncertain terms what he thought of me, with the last words shouting 'The next fucking time I see you I am going to fucking kill you fucking shit bag'

The sister of the casualty department came out to see what was going and saw this man being led away by the police, she said to me 'I see your bedroom manner is still not up to scratch yet'

Well that wasn't the end of this man; we were called to St. Albans Abbey about two months later. Along with us, we had a local news paper reporter who was given permission to ride out with us to see the workings of the ambulance service and write

"A day in the life of an Ambulance man"

We arrived at the Abbey to find this male laying on the ground saying he was having a heart attack. I am looking at this man and again I am thinking this doesn't look right, we loaded him onto the ambulance and looking at him again I said

'You're the man who said the next time you saw me you were going to kill me'

Well that was a big mistake, this man who was at deaths door one minute leaped off the stretcher and went for me. So I was right I thought (I am quick like that), the reporter couldn't believe what was happening in front of him. There I am fighting with this man, calling out to my driver to get the police, to get to the hospital at the same time. At the hospital we were met by the same police crew who took him off the first time. As they took him off me they said 'We thought you ambulance bods were here to help poor people in distress not to fight them'

But that's only after they fought with him, getting him into their police car!

Sitting in our control room one night at about 0300 a call came into control that a person had taken an overdose of tablets in a cottage next to a big house near a Ministry of Defence establishment. It was not our call but we were passing the time talking to the controllers on duty (all two of them) The ambulance was dispatched to the location and that was that we thought, until the ambulance called up to say it was at the location but couldn't move as it was stuck. It was a lucky time for us as the fire service had just purchased a tow truck rescue type vehicle. So they were sent to the location to pull this ambulance out of the what ever. It was recovered by the rescue truck. The Sub officer who was on the rescue truck came back from the job, and came into the control to tell us the story of what had happened to this ambulance.

The ambulance had arrived at the scene and seen the light on, at the cottage next to a big house, and headed straight towards the cottage. Being a frosty night the crew thought the ground was all asphalt because it was completely covered in frost. Unknown to them it was not asphalt, but a lawn and the ambulance was stuck right up to its axel.

As the rescue truck was winching it of the grass, a window opened from the big house and man shouts out 'I say what's going on down there?'

The sub officer replied 'It's an ambulance stuck on your lawn and we are just winching it off we are nearly finished'

'Oh ok' The man replies,

Shuts the window and immediately reopens it shouting

'I am Rear Admiral (name) that's no lawn, that's my Fucking Croquet lawn'

Oops they thought. And the fire service sub officer couldn't stop laughing nor could the crew. The Rear Admiral appeared from the house, in his dressing gown, and walked over to fire truck and demanded to know what an earth was going on there and who was in charge? The sub officer steps forward and says he was the senior person there.

'Good, so why have you chosen my croquet lawn to park this "Thing" on' As he points to the ambulance

He then went on with out stopping for breath and told them in no uncertain terms.

'You will all be hearing from my department first thing in the morning mark my words'

They said for some unknown reason they all stood to attention and nearly saluted as he stormed off back into his house.

You can imagine the cost even in those days was several thousand pounds to put the croquet lawn back to its proper playing condition again!

I had a knack at imitating accents and could do quite a good Northern Ireland one.

I walked into our local outpatients department and saw one of my colleagues from my station and said to him in a Northern Irish accent 'you've got three minutes to get out there's a bomb'

Quietly so I thought. A woman who was sitting down in front of us overheard and in her broad Northern Irish accent said 'I don't think that's very funny'

We both had to get out of the department quick because we were dying of laughter.

Another trick we learnt to do, but it could only done with the Bedford J's ambulances. We would turn the ignition off, let it freewheel but leave it in gear and switch the ignition back on. After about thirty yards, this would cause a build up of gas in the exhaust it would ignite and make a big bang. My colleague loved to do it especially if he saw a lose dog walking along the pavement! They would run off so fast it was incredible to watch them go. Thinking back it was very cruel

Bruce and I coming back from a London hospital one night travelling down Tottenham Court road saw this young couple walking arm in arm towards us. I did the turning the key trick! Well he must have thought it was a bomb going off, he jumped into the air and his girl friend caught him in her arms as he came down! We had to stop the ambulance because the tears of laughter were just running down our cheeks! Childish I know but it was one way to let off stress.

Following one industrial disputes we were awarded an extra 25p a week if we carried out maintenance or diagnosed faults on our ambulances. That was too much for our Chief and he refused to pay it. So the first time we broke down in the ambulance we informed our control, who asked, 'What was wrong with the ambulance.'

I replied 'I am not allowed to say, but I will give you a clue, bring plenty of water.'   The problem was a top hose had gone on the radiator, but no 25p then no information.. So when the engineer turned up, he was a very unhappy chappie, that I wouldn't tell control what the problem was. So he had to go all the way back to the station to get a hose to fit. But we had a laugh playing cat and mouse with our control over breakdowns, but we never did get our 25p.

There were always stories running wild within the service, but the only one I could vouch for was, an ambulance going into Brigade workshops. It was having a major over haul, when the fitters noticed that part of the roofs paintwork was not the right colour. As they inspected the area they found that they could put their hand through the roof. The story goes that whilst it was going into a car park the barrier was just not high enough to let the ambulance go under, the corner of the ambulance roof hit the barrier with some force. The fibre glass roof was badly damaged, so the crew set about repairing the damage themselves so not to get into any trouble. They used cardboard and paper mache and found some paint in almost the same shade of the original colour.

No one owned up to this incident, so the whole station staff of only eight staff got an official warning.

Moving none NHS items on our ambulances was not common practice, but now and again needs must and all that! One of our colleagues, from our station, made promotion, to Assistant Chief Officer. Which in it self was not remarkable, but he had to deal with a disciplinary hearings, (which made us made us laugh on our station). An L/a was caught for transporting a motor bike in an Ambulance one night. That was not the only thing that he was disciplined for, but that was the main charge.

This L/a, was dismissed from the service. Our laughter was because some years previously the now Assistant Chief, whilst driving a sitting car decided to move a donkey he owned from one field in St.Albans to another field some miles away in a sitting car, we all thought that was a laugh at the time. But he got away with it and now he had dismissed someone for gross misconduct for transporting a none NHS item!

One of our other crews was sent to do an admission from home address to a hospital just over the county border. The crew noticed in a lay-by, a couple of radiators, which he could do with, in his house. They unloaded their patient at the hospital as quickly as possible, and headed back to the lay-by to pick up the radiators and put them in the back of the ambulance..

Heading back to base they got another call, because the other on duty ambulance (us) had been dispatched to another call. So they stopped unloaded the radiators and went off to deal with their call. After unloading their patient they headed back to where they had placed the radiators, on their arrival much to their disgust some one had nicked them! We never did hear the last of their moaning that they had been robbed!

Every year we had to be measured for a new uniform. If we missed being measured by the tailor, we had to submit a form with our measurements on, and these were posted onto the uniform supplier. This was duly done by one old boy L/a. Some two months later up turned our uniforms, and our L/a s trousers were very short long trousers! They were about ten inches too short. How an earth did that happen we asked and he explained how he had done the measuring to make such a mistake. He showed us how he did the measuring. He got the tape to do the inside leg measurement and as he couldn't see the measurement he opened up his legs and bent his knees to reach the bottom of the tape! Putting his thumb on the tape at floor level to save the measurement! We said that's how your trousers are too short, it took him about twenty seconds to realise his mistake. We just fell about laughing

On occasions, we had to be escorted by the police to hospital in London, these were only used in life or death cases, and it also insured we had a non stop journey to the hospital.

On one such journey to the, Westminster children's hospital, in London. The Metropolitan police had organised an escort, they were brilliant at them. Having been met by a police motorcyclist on a Valacett at Elstree on the A5, as we were entering Edgware a Bedford van driver took no notice of the policeman on his bike or us either, so the policeman starts banging on the side of the van to gain the attention of the driver! Still no response from the driver, so the policeman pulls up along the side door and gets hold of the door handle and slides it open! That did the trick the last we saw of him was going up the grass verge towards a brick wall!

There was a police presence at every traffic light and then two police cars took over our escort, as we approached Grosvenor Place in the centre of London we got held up by a removal lorry that nearly rammed us in the side, he had ignored the police to stop, the driver started shouting at me, then I saw in my wing mirror my colleague open the side window of the ambulance and punched him straight in the face just as I managed to move off. After handing the child over to the hospital I caught up with one of the policemen who had escorted us, to tell him what had happened.

'Well son lets put it this way I saw him head butt your mates hand!'

That was good enough for me, as we went off laughing.

I had to interview potential staff for a new position in our service, we called these staff Auxiliary ambulance staff. They were employed to pick up patients from their home address, and convey them to the new Geriatric day units that were being set up in hospitals within Hertfordshire. This was a good way for some staff to start their careers within the service. If they could cope with dealing with this kind of work they would make very good ambulance staff, and quite a few of them went on to work as full time ambulance staff. Several have successfully gone on to being paramedics and then some to be Officers.

We operated this interview by having an open door system. We put an advert in the local paper saying the kind of people were looking for and they could turn at the ambulance station between

0930/1630hrs.on a particular day. On their arrival they were met by our training schools driving instructor who would check their driving licence to ensure it didn't have any points on it. Then he would take them out for a quick driving test, on passing that they were given an application to fill in. If they were unsuitable they were told they could come back and try again in six months time if they saw another advert.

There was a perfume that was on the market at the time called Poison I hated the smell of this perfume and nearly every-other woman I interviewed was wearing it

On one of these interviews at Welwyn Garden City station, Jack the driving instructor came in with a mans application form and said

'I am not sure about this man he is strange.'

As he left my office he said

'Over to you' and laughed.

'Cheers'

I said as he walked out to bring the man into my office. I introduced myself, and then went through his application form with him. I asked him what school he went to as it was not on the form. He replied it was 'local',

'Ok, can you be more specific'

He mentioned one I knew, so I wrote in the appropriate box on the form. 'Did you get any qualifications'

'No' came the reply.

I then looked at the box asking what was his previous employment or present employer. It was a local glue company which two years previously I remembered as I was reading his form, there had been a serious incident there.

'Haven't you been employed since this date two years ago and why did you leave?'

'Well let's put it this way I didn't get on with the people' He replied.

I have now made up my mind he was not the kind of person we were looking for in this kind of job, so I turned over the page just to carry on and then get rid of him. The question in the first box on this page was, have you had a criminal conviction spent or still on-going?, to which he had replied yes! The next question, what was the conviction was for? His written reply was prison!

'You haven't put down what was the conviction for' I asked

He replied 'I'd rather not say'

'Well you have been honest up to now so why can't you say why you spent time in prison'

After a long pause he replied 'I stabbed someone and they died at the place I worked at.'

That's right I remember now (I thought to myself) my old work mate was telling me about the incident when it happened two years ago that's how I remember the incident.

I asked 'What made you come for this job, as it entails getting on with elderly people who can be extremely difficult at times.'

'I was told to come by my probation officer'

This shocked me even more, how any one with a grain of intelligence could tell this man, who clearly was totally unsuitable to deal with, or mix with, any kind of people let alone be told to come and apply for a position such as this.

I thanked him for coming along I told him 'I don't think this kind of work is for you, but if you could ask your probation officer to talk to me about this I would be pleased to discuss anything with him.'

I gave him my card to pass on to his probation officer. What also struck me as strange as he left me was how he was out of prison in two years after murdering some one. That probation officer never did contact me, and luckily for him or her they didn't because if they had, they would have got more than ear full!

How could any one in there right mind and supposedly a professional person at that, send someone so totally unsuitable for this kind of job is beyond my comprehension, or as the saying goes "Is it me?" Still Jack and I had a bloody good laugh over it.

Dealing with complaints made by members of the public or from patients or patients relatives can be testing at times not for the genuine complainant but for some people who like to have a moan and as the years went on more and more people moan just for the sake of it.

Our service policy in dealing with complaints was to visit the complainant so we could sit face to face and see what was really behind the complaint. Also the service thought it was a better way in communicating with the complainant rather than an impersonal letter sent out, plus also you get to the real nub of the problem.

Let's be honest here, for someone to complain either from a patient's point of view or from a relative view on how we treated the patient takes a lot of doing. Not only have they had the trauma of the incident they have suffered but also spending time in hospital, then to come home and put pen to paper. After visiting the complainant we always followed up with a letter highlighting the problems that we had discussed together and hope that a solution was found and any remedy for the future.

As I have already said most of them were not our fault but if we found out that the compliant was justified in the way patients were treated by our staff I would come down hard on those members of staff. I was not called the "Smiling assassin" for nothing

As progress marches forward from the Bell, to the Two Tone Horns, and now to the Sirens. We can be heard be the world and his dog. That became too much for one man living in Dunstable. He started writing letters of complaint about our new Toy (sirens) as he put it. These things are too noisy, and they were being used for the sake of it, and he wanted the ambulance service to have the staff stopped immediately in using them. I sent the station officer responsible for that area to visit this man. He came back from the meeting and walked into my officer sat down in a heap and said

'This one is going to last and last for years!'

'What'.

He went on to say. 'This man lives on the main road between Dunstable and Luton'

'Well I know that because of the address on the letter'

'Hang on, hang on, the point is, he lives on the cross roads where there is a set of traffic lights!'

'Ah I see'

We just looked at each other for about 10 seconds in silence.

'So what and how have you left it'

'I hate you some times boss, well actually most of the time' he replied

'Well I know that but you will just have to join the queue of other well wishers.'

He said I tried to explain to him the use of the sirens, and why they were fitted and unfortunately the location of his house being at a busy cross road with traffic lights. Then finally with the hospital only being a mile up the road from him it was going to be inevitable that sirens would be used there. It was something that would not be resolved. The complainants replied 'That was it was not good enough'

The value of his house had dropped because of all this disruption caused by all this noise. I also asked him if he has complained to the police and fire service about the use of their sirens but he declined to respond to that question.

Now with the best will in the world I could understand we were going to have problems with this gentleman. The main point he had pointed out was that his house had been devalued so he said. I said we would send him a letter explaining every thing discussed that day, but emphasized that the use of the sirens are used only in extreme circumstances, going to the hospital, and other times they are used for safety of other road users especially at traffic lights. As with all letters, they had to be signed off by the Chief Ambulance officer. Hoping he might pass on some words of wisdom on the subject, or perhaps point us in another direction to tackle the problem.

No such luck, so off went the letter to this gentleman explaining the ambulance services position on this matter. Sure enough my officer was right, the gentleman started to phone us when the sirens were used outside his house. It was going to be a no win situation between either of us, as I tried to explain to him over the phone, he refused to see me. I said we cannot stop using these sirens, and if you talk to police or fire service, I am sure you will get the same response. Unfortunately it's up to you, how you are going to deal with it. I do sympathies with you. But he hit back saying you are not the one living here and I don't want your sympathy I want action, which I could understand. It did die a death in the end and I never heard anymore after about four months.

Peoples perception can be somewhat distorted as I tried to deal with another complainant. This was different about an ambulance having been parked in the grounds of Hemel Hempstead hospital for over four hours without moving! In his letter he said that he had taken his wife into the hospital for an outpatient's appointment at 0930hrs. When I came out of the building the ambulance was still parked there, not having moved an inch, from where I had first seen it when I had arrived. You cannot go bleating on about the lack of resources if you allow your crews to hide for all this time. He also put the registration of the ambulance.

This I thought would be a easy one to resolve, all I had to do was get hold of the journey sheet for the ambulance on that day, see what the crew had been doing in its movements and go and see the complainant. I got the journey sheet for the ambulance that the complainant had given us the registration. The first thing I look for is the crew names, as far as I was concerned these two were a very good crew. I also checked with the control manager, to see what work they had carried out for that day in case they had not completed the journey sheet correctly. They had transferred a patient at 0945hrs from a ward in the same building as the OPD, and transferred the patient to the Royal Free hospital in Hampstead. The crew returned the nurse back to the ward along with equipment arriving back at 12.33 hrs. I checked the mileage and checked that the work had been under taken and the times corresponded with the computer timings. All appeared correct from the services point of view and mine, I could blow this man out of the water.

So I duly turn up at the gentleman's house having first made an appointment to meet him and to discuss his complaint. He was not really pleased to see me as he said he thought having some one to come around to his house to see him was a another waste of resources. I thought, Here we go another person who writes a letter and is beginning to regret his actions. I explained how the service treats all complaints the same, how we take them all seriously enough to insure the complainant is seen, and try to put right, quickly if it is deemed necessary. I showed him all the evidence on the journey sheet that the crew had filled in when they move off the station. This showed that the vehicle had moved and what times it had carried out the journey, but the name of the patient and crew were erased.

To my amazement he said 'You are lying and so is your crew and your control is in league with them. This is disgraceful that you come here, you a senior officer are sitting in my house and trying to twist what I have said. I can assure you that I am a member of the local heath watch dog and I will press on with this'

He went on to say 'The next time I go into the hospital with my wife I will photograph each wheel of a stationary ambulance to show that the wheels have not moved by the valves on the wheels.'

I must admit that I was taken aback by this mans attitude

He went onto say 'I will show you that you are wasting money by having ambulance sitting at the hospital doing nothing'.

I had to say to him that we were not going to agree on anything here today, and I was very sorry that I was not able to reassure him that a journey had been undertaken. And for some reason you think I am covering up some major fraud. His wife did not say a word the whole time I was there, and I didn't get offered a cup of tea either! It was no use in trying to explain to him about the service workings, because I believe he had some mental health issues. These were beginning to show as he got more worked up about the issue. Still it was another talking point with my weekly prayer meetings with my officers, and leg pulling that I was the biggest fraud in the service and had been found out at last. It's nice to have such supportive staff.

After a visit to the A&E dept., at St. Albans I was driving back to my station in my staff car when a car shot across my path at a road junction, causing me to brake hard to avoid a collision. I thought I must have words with this young man who was with his girl friend. Knowing he was going into an unmade road I thought he must live in this road and would be stopping soon. I got to the house as this young couple were walking up to the front door of a house. I asked him if he aware that his actions could have resulted in him and his girl friend and myself enjoying hospital food for a couple days. In fairness to him he apologised straight away and really he was a very pleasant young man. Imagine my surprise when watching TV some time later seeing this young man winning a Formule 1 Grand Prix race! Also in the crowd was his girlfriend who was now his wife.

Doctors and relatives come up with strange diagnosis, which make us check our first aid manuals.

Having to deal with a 19 year old boy who had to go into hospital, with as the doctor had given a diagnosis of stomach problems? Whist we waited for the young man to get all his suit case packed, his mother said 'I don't know what the doctor is playing at I having been telling him for some time now I know the problem with my son'

We both asked her at the same 'Oh what's that'

'Its his uterus'

As she brings her right hand and touches her left shoulder blade explaing were the problem was.

My old boy mate and I looked at each other, and he said to her 'no wonder he is poorly with that problem'

Another call to a man with a temperature, this was the doctor reason for calling an ambulance. As we entered the bedroom, the man was standing in the corner facing the wall whistling like a canary! I turned and asked his wife how long has he been like this. She replied 'About three hours'

My old boy mate asked. 'What did the doctor say when he saw your husband like this'

'Oh his got a temperature I will send him to hospital and see why he his burning up like this, and promptly left.

My colleague told her. 'He's got pneumonia that's why he is like this'

Oh that's funny, he only saw a chiropodist the other day so I don't think its that'

Biting our lips my mate said. 'No perhaps your right'

CHAPTER 8:
Ambulance accidents

With the distances we had to travel and the traffic we had to deal with, it's inevitable that we had accidents within the service. In our service we often had to travel up to 30 miles or more to hospital. Also the increase of hospital to hospital emergency transfer stretches the resources even further. Towards the end of my career in the service, with the lack of Intensive Care beds at hospitals, we were transferring patients well over 100 miles to other hospitals. I also had my share of accidents along with those I also had to investigate as an officer. The drivers in most cases are suspended from driving until we have been informed that no prosecution for the accident is being sought by the police.

All ambulances are very well maintained, having a service every six thousand miles or six weeks which ever comes first. It is the driver's responsibility to check the tyres at the start of each shift. The ambulance has a working life of seven years or one hundred and forty thousand miles which ever comes first.

I have been extremely proud of my crews in their professional approach when they have had an accident. Without exception they have always alighted from the ambulance and treated the patient from the other vehicle until back up has arrived on the scene. They were then taken to hospital by me or their station officer for a check up or for debriefing back at station. All drivers involved in serious accident were suspended to allow investigation to be carried out by ourselves and the police. The police always carried out their job in a very professional and impartial manner.

I count my self fortunate, as my accidents were of a relative minor nature. We all had to fill in a form called an H.A.S. 71. The form was A4 two sided and had same the questions that all insurance forms asked. We used to say if you are going to have an accident have a big one, at least you could write "IT'S A WRITE OFF" rather than all the little bits of damage here, there and every where. Every time someone had an accident we were awarded a medal, called a 71 club medal made by one of the "old boys". But if we didn't have any accidents we got a proper award issued by ROSPA I think I got the odd two or three or four I cannot remember!!

I had all the minor bumps and scrapes whilst driving on emergency calls. My only big accident whilst I was driving was at 0130 hrs. Whilst were enroute to a RTA on the M1 going along a fast stretch of the A5, well as fast as you could in a Bedford J as we approached Redbourn a small village were you could see up the hill into this village with no problems at all.

A car pulled out from a minor road to my left about 200 yards in front of me, no problem I thought, keep flashing my headlights at him and he might see me! I had to do this with my foot, because we didn't have automatic flashing lights in those days. We also had the problem of our blue light in those days, being small and in the middle of the roof of the ambulance and like our bells, past their sell by date.

I pulled over to the right hand side of the road, foot on the head light switch, on off, on off, I had just reached the rear of this car, and without warning he turns right across the front of my ambulance, colliding with him right in the offside rear of his Austin A40 as I tried to avoid him. I went onto the pavement, up an embankment into a massive brick and stone wall and came to rest in the front garden of someone's house.

My colleague and I got out of the ambulance shaken but unhurt and ran over to see the occupant of the A40. He was still sitting in the car and as we opened the door he said 'I never saw you where did you come from'

I was so bloody annoyed that I never answered. I went back to our ambulance to radio control that we had been involved in accident and were unable to proceed to the M1, One year later I had to go to court, so that blame could be apportioned by the insurance companies can recover their costs for the damage to the vehicles. It was deemed by the judge as 50/50 accident. I should not have been overtaking at a junction, and the car driver should have been more aware on what was going on at that time in the morning.

One big accident I was involved in as a passenger turned into a very bizarre and a very twisting story, something that you would not believe. When I was told about the whole story, I was astonished as nothing has ever come close to this in my remaining years in the service.

It started out as a normal transfer of a girl of 11 years of age from our local hospital at St.Albans to Mount Vernon Hospital plastic unit about 25 miles away. The mother was going to travel with us, but she was running late so we left the hospital without her. It had been very dry for about six weeks with no rainfall at all, and it just starting to rain only very lightly. As we were going along I was talking to the nurse and the girl trying to find out what had caused her injury.

I began to get concerned about my crew mates driving as we seemed to be going too fast for the condition of the roads. There was no need to be rushing as this was just a simple transfer. I remember moving off the centre seat to sit opposite the patient, as I did that, I felt the ambulance start to slide, then go into a spin hitting the kerb and rolling onto its side, it slide into a brick wall of a garden.. The patient fell on top of me and I saw the carry chair fall off the rear door hitting the nurse on her back, as you can imagine it all happened so quickly but very slowly and very clearly all at the same time.

My driver managed to get out of the cab, and along with some passers by, got the rear doors open of the ambulance, while we are still lying in a heap in the rear of the ambulance. I didn't want to move, in case the girl was injured who was still laying on top of me. She was crying her eyes out and screaming all at the same time right in my ear! The nurse was motionless as the weight of the carry chair had severely stunned her and as she was a very slight thing you could see she was badly injured. I never moved until another ambulance turned up with our station officer to assist in moving these patients into another ambulance. They were both taken back to St Albans hospital which we had just left, to be examined by the casualty doctor.

My colleague and I were taken back to our station by our station officer to be interviewed by him and the police to give statements and fill in all the accident forms.

I was off work for over 6 months with severe back pain and had to attend physiotherapy three times a week.

During the time I was off I went to visit the injured girl and her parents at their home. I thought I would see how she was getting on. The mother told me the whole story from when she was first injured and what subsequently happened to her daughter.

It started on a Friday, her daughter had received a chain letter, saying if you don't pass this letter on you will have an accident within twenty four hours and die within forty eight hours. Her mother told her to destroy the letter as they were rubbish. The girl then went out on her bike up to the village centre to meet up with her friends. The front brakes on her bike came loose and jammed into her front wheel throwing her, over the handle bars breaking her jaw and she had cuts and abrasions to her body. She was then taken to hospital where she was kept in for the week end. Then the hospital decided to send her to Mount Vernon Hospital.

You came along on the Monday to convey her to the plastics hospital to have her jaw repaired. Whist enroute you overturned your ambulance, and she went back to the hospital to be checked over. Whilst she was being wheeled up to the X-ray department on a trolley the wheel came off and she fell off onto the ground. She now getting very hysterical and was only calmed down by me (her mum) and the nursing staff. She kept reminding me about the letter they had destroyed, and she thought she would die very soon. The X-ray was taken and it appeared she had a fractured collar bone. The casualty doctor did not believe this, and asked for the X Ray to be taken again and the second time the fracture was not there!

During her stay over night in hospital, her mother said it was decided that they would convey her to the plastic unit themselves, because there was no way she could persuade her to go in an ambulance. As they arrived at Mount Vernon hospital her husband carried her into the ward, and her daughter said that she could not se anything. They told the ward sister what she had just said, they did a quick test to make sure she was telling the truth, and it appeared that she was. They told us not to worry about this at the moment so we told them the story of what had happened to her so far,

After listening to this story they called in an ophthalmic specialist to come to see her, he gave her a clean bill of health as far as her eyes were concerned, but said they would do more test at Moorfields eye hospital in London. They would only carry out these tests, when she had fully recovered from the surgery. These further tests were carried out and the only conclusion they came to was that she had gone hysterically blind, and her sight would come back to her over a period of time.

I visited them again after a further 6 months and her mother had good news for me. Whilst they had been on holiday they were on the beach and her daughter was with her brother playing and suddenly she jumped up saying she could see!

I was really pleased for the whole family as they had been through a great ordeal for over nine months and they never once complained about the ambulance service or the hospital in the way things had gone so badly wrong for them.

After being off work for six months because of this accident I returned to work, I was a passenger again, minding my own business going back to our station for lunch. When a car going at about 35 mph came out of a side road and rammed us straight in the side of ambulance. We were spun in a complete 360 degrees, we travelled backwards up the road before coming to a complete stop, watching the car driver being thrown out of his car by the sheer force of the impact of the collision. He bounced onto the road and did several somersaults before lying in a heap. We ran over to him, he was deeply unconscious from a head injury, then he started to fit, we tended to him until another ambulance conveyed him to hospital. He was in hospital only 36 hours before discharging himself. The police caught up with him at his home, because they found out he did not have a driving licence, also no insurance and the car should not have been on the road because it was not roadworthy. I was off for another month of sickness with a back injury again.

Unfortunately there were occasions when we were involved in fatal accidents. Almost all these accidents involve an overtaking manoeuvre

We had two fatal accidents involving ambulance staff whilst I was in the service.

The first one was just as I had joined the ambulance brigade. It was an ambulance from a neighbouring station called to the M1 junction seven on a dark and foggy night. Whist loading a patient from an earlier RTA onto their ambulance a Jaguar car being driven by a male hit a road works machine, then collided into the ambulance crew loading the stretcher into the ambulance, killing one ambulance man and seriously injuring the patient and the other ambulance man.

The other member of staff who was killed in an RTA, was a leading ambulance man driving a sitting car, for some unknown reason he collided with a railway bridge in Welwyn Garden City. There were no mechanical faults found on the sitting car, or any medical reasons why this should have happened.

One crew proceeding to an RTA, in Harpenden were within 300 yards of the incident they began to overtake the stationary traffic held up by the accident. Suddenly from the driver's left hand side a car shot out in between the stationary cars and the ambulance hit the car broadside on. The car carried on across the road onto a grass common throwing the passengers out of the car as it went on for quite a little distance before coming to a stop in some bushes. Several people died in this car. It appeared that the driver's foot got trapped on the accelerator as the car was an automatic it kept on going.

What made it even more tragic, their child, was getting married the next day, and they had been setting up the hall for the wedding reception.

Another ambulance on route to a 999 call in Dunstable involved overtaking, the car drove out into the path of the ambulance from the driver's right hand side, and he was unable to avoid colliding with it. The driver knew instantly that he had caused serious injury to the child who was sitting in the near side back seat of the car. The car was being driven by the child's mother who was only slightly injured. The crew worked hard trying to save the life of this child until relieved by another crew and by one of my officers who travelled in the ambulance to the hospital. Unfortunately the child died. Any call involving a child's death always causes anguish to ambulance crews.

The ambulance man was praised for his and his crew members actions by all that had witnessed the accident. He was also exonerated from any blame for the accident. Not that it helped the child or the family.

Sunday afternoon. An ambulance had been dispatched from Welwyn Garden City out of its own station area, which now has become the norm with the amount of calls they now have to deal with.

As they entered St. Albans having travelled well over 10 miles, and approaching a line of traffic, they begun to overtake the cars that had pulled over to let them overtake, as they got to the head of the queue a car turned right across their path, they could not avoid the collision and the young car driver unfortunately died. The crew did all they could for the driver but to no avail. One of the crew was severely traumatised from the experience of this incident, and was never the same person again. He moved on to other positions within the service as he couldn't cope with driving any more, but all this failed and he left the service.

One accident had management scratching its heads. A crew from St. Albans were sent to a golf course male collapsed.

Control got a call 'Could you send another ambulance our windscreen has come out! And we are unable to proceed'

Control duly sent another ambulance and the duty ambulance officer on call to sort out the problem. On his arrival not only had the windscreen "Come out" the ambulance appeared to be bent up from underneath upwards like a banana! It had to be recovered by a low loader to workshops.

On the Monday we started to investigate what had happened because the ambulance had to be written off. Three officers including the assistant chief officer and I went to the location and started to measure up the site of the accident. It appeared that the ambulance had came over the brow of hump from which they took off and landed some fifty feet from this hump and carried on for a considerable distance. In the statement they made after their return to station, they said they were travelling at about 10 to 15 miles an hour. This appeared to be far from the truth. I had a very good friend in the police service and I asked him if it was possible to work out the speed the ambulance was travelling at, allowing for the fact they were travelling on grass. He came back to me to say that the calculations showed that even allowing for the ambulance being in the air and then the distance that they had travelled along the grass it must have been in the region of 45mph to 50mph! Much faster than the crew had said and that's why the ambulance was so severely damaged. There was some suspicion that the driver had been drinking but we were not in a position to prove it. The crew were disciplined and the driver receiving a final written warning whist his colleague received a written warning.

CHAPTER 9:
Reflections/Achievements

As I have said before I have been lucky in my years in the service and most of my achievements have been down to team work. I hoped my legacy was that I was seen as fair in dealing with staff, communicating with them. I did have the nick name "The Smiling Assassin", this was because I was always smiling but if the need arose I had to discipline or even had to dismiss staff. This was only one of many names they called me I am sure!

Several members of staff are also mentioned who have carried heroic achievements

My wife Valerie has had to put up with more than her share of being on her own or hearing me whittling on, or in some cases losing my temper over the phone to some one.

So I was extremely pleased, and also unbeknown to me, when she received a letter from the Lord Chamberlain, Buckingham Palace. The Lord Chamberlain is commanded by Her Majesty to invite her to a Garden party at Buckingham Palace On Tuesday 22 July 1997. By some chance I could pop along as well!

Each service Chief Officer gets a request each year from the Lord Chamberlain office asking if they would like to nominate a person to attend a garden party at the Palace. This task is normally quite easy as the Chief normally nominates the longest serving ambulance person in their service.

It was an absolutely glorious day, when we arrived to the allotted parking place. I got out of the car and started to put my uniform jacket and cap on. A group of French school children were walking past and stopped and ask me if I knew the Queen? Also was I going to tea with her? And was I a General? I had to smile, and to their disappointment I told them I was only an Ambulance man and not a General and we were off to the Queens party. The teacher said thank you for stopping to talk to them, it had still made their day that they had met someone who was going to see the Queen! And something they could to tell their family when they got home.

The weather was sweltering hot, the food was brilliant you could eat and drink (tea) as much as you wanted, we could walk all around the gardens at Buckingham Palace, and we saw some very famous people and got very close to all the Royal family. We had a wonderful time.

My wife really enjoyed the day and I hope it repaid some of the frustrating times she had and still has with me.

Some of the other things I achieved happened mostly because I was a union shop steward. On night shifts I would read the Whitley Council hand book on pay and conditions, this was because I was bored. On nights sometimes on the Borehamwood station we never went out for the whole week of nights even though Bruce and I would try and volunteer for work but it helped me to get to sleep quicker!

One of the things I had read in this booklet was, it appeared we were not receiving the proper payments when working overtime on night shifts at week ends. When I brought this to the attention of our Chief Officer you could have heard a pin drop, and if he could have, he would have had me shot there and then. This involved several years of back pay to us all, and a considerable amount of money for the ambulance service to find and pay out! After some time and gnashing of teeth we all got the money!

As well as the replacement of bells to two tone horns we also managed to get two blue lights fitted to the roof of our ambulances front and rear although this did take longer to achieve. This came with the help from a very friendly police officer who pointed me in the direction of the road traffic act, which said a rotating blue light must be seen from three hundred and sixty degrees. When you opened the sky light on the Bedford J it could not be seen from the rear. I won the day, but the two blue lights would only be fitted to new ambulances.

I remember one meeting with our chief I brought up the subject of buying a device for lifting patients off the ground, following trauma. This was an American device, as most good ideas were; it was called a scoop stretcher. It's an aluminium stretcher that's unclips at the top and bottom of the stretcher so that you can put the two halves either side of the patient, then you would slide these underneath the body clipping the top and bottom together so you could lift the patient off the floor without causing more damage to the patient. My chief listened to me and after a brief thought said

'No Hertfordshire is too hilly!'

Even now thinking about it, makes me laugh.

Trying to get equipment for the ambulances was always a problem and when the Rotary club approached me, saying they were willing to raise funds to buy lifepack 5 Heart monitors difibulators. The Harpenden and St.Albans Rotary club and the Lions clubs joined in as well and if they were successful, the British Heart Foundation would supply one as well. Through all their hard work, they raised sufficient funds to place three sets onto our ambulances in St. Albans, for which we were extremely appreciative.

A collective achievement by staff, country wide obtained better training, and professionalism. This all came about through having to go on strike. I can assure you not one of us wanted to go on strike, but this was the only way we were going to achieve our goal. Our pay and condition were the same as all county council manual employees. It was not only the pay that concerned us all, we had to have better training. We knew we could do more for the patients we attended to, and the days of training with the St John was long outdated to our needs.

This was only achieved, after a long struggle, we got regional training schools for better training in emergency aid and proper instruction on driving. Some years later more strikes took place and this led to the introduction of paramedics that they now have today. Whilst this took time to achieve all this, and the sacrifice staff gave was worth it. And I must stress that this does not in any shape or form dismiss the achievements and the dedication carried out by ambulance staff prior to all this training.

I have already mentioned earlier "Jones" the ambulance man who dropped the light. Later he went on to be a control officer. As an ambulance man he was an excellent example of how to treat and look after people. He had a bad experience when he was in the Army stationed in Palestine. He was on patrol in his army truck when it passed a lorry loaded with oranges. It exploded trapping him for sometime in his truck under all these oranges. From that day on if he saw or smelt an orange he fled from it.

He was sent to an RTA just outside Radlett on the A5, where a Corvett Stingray, being driven by the Chief Executive from General Motors had crashed. It was the first one in the U.K. to be used as a demonstrator. I was the second ambulance to arrive at this RTA. Jones had just loaded his ambulance with the American who was seriously injured. Jones colleague waited for our arrival and told us that this mans wife was still in the car with leg injuries, but was not to serious. They said they were now leaving and would meet up with us at RNO Stanmore hospital. We treated her for several fractures and cuts and abrasions although not serious we conveyed her to RNO Stanmore to be with her husband. After we passed over our patient into the care of the causality unit, we talked to Jones and his mate about the accident. He told us that his patient had been thrown out of the car and suffered serious injuries.

My colleague went to the hospital a couple of days later and spoke to the causality sister and asked how the patients from our RTA were doing. She told us that if it hadn't been for the careful treatment and handling by Jones he would never have walked again or even worse he could be dead. He suffered two fractures of the vertebrae and multiple fractures of the legs. A fracture of the neck which only needed the wrong movement when being moved and it would have been a disaster. This was all done before the days of spinal boards, neck collars and all the training that comes when treating a spinal injury. Jones in his usual modest way when I mentioned it to him said 'Well I knew it was some kind of spinal injury so just treated him accordingly'

I must mention an ambulance man who gave his life trying to save a policeman who had been called to an incident in Leicester. This ambulance man had been called to the scene of this incident to pick up a policeman who had been shot. With the police they devised a plan to pick the injured policeman up. He and his colleague drove the ambulance to get as close as they could to the policeman using the ambulance for protection, they tried to get the policeman into the ambulance, but the gunman opened fire, killing one of the ambulance men. I along with a junior officer and the Assistant Chief Ambulance officer attended his funereal in Leicester.

I always said to my self if I was ever promoted I would try and keep staff informed of what was happing within the service. I had seen and experienced too much of the secret service I had joined the service for the patient's sake and not my own. I told staff that many times over, that we were not there to have pony club badges on our shoulders or scrambled egg on our caps.(Rank markings and Braid) The public are not interested in that or even know what the rank markings are for anyway. They want some one who is going to help them in their hour of need. I remember on one of my interviews I was asked by a member of the board of interviewers,

'One American President had on his desk a plaque saying The Buck Stops Here. If you had a plaque on your desk what would yours say?'

I replied 'Communication'

I encouraged meetings with my officers, who also took this on board and they held regular meetings with their junior officers. When I took over the responsibility of the control staff I encouraged them to attend the operational meetings as well, because the control had a big impact on day to day staff issues. They had always been left out of the loop. I also thought no one-person has all the answers. I would look forward to criticism to insure things could be achieved. Taking on board one Chief Ambulance officers remarks at a conference 'The ambulance service is only as good as the ambulance person who knocks on a patient's door'

He was Hundred percent correct because that's how the general public first see us, and judge us.

I must mention the Control, or Dispatch the new term which was being introduced as I was leaving the service. This is the hub of the ambulance service, where all the calls for an ambulance go into, then distributed out. In the past this was a dumping ground for staff with bad backs, bad sickness record, or any body who had given up on emergency work. They were put there whether they were suitable or not. There were a few good controllers who worked their socks off and supported the other control room staff.

When I first started in the service in Hertfordshire there were four separate control rooms to receive the calls for an ambulance and to mobilize the ambulances to the calls. These calls were all written down on paper forms, and put in index box where the calls were tracked. The controller had to remember, what each ambulance was doing and where it was going. This system worked well at the time but as time went on, with the reduction to one control room for Hertfordshire, and ever increasing calls year on year. Which were increasing by at least 5% per annum.

The service started looking at new technology that was arising. The computer age was coming. Experts who were called in to make up a programme, said at the time it was more difficult to work out a programme for mobilising ambulances, than landing and taking off aircraft at Heathrow Airport!

Now there is only one control room for the whole of Beds & Herts. It is a highly sophisticated technological department and is, as highly stressful as being out on the road. They were dealing with, when I left, over 400,-999 calls a day and over 180 doctor or hospital calls a day. Whilst ambulance staff can only do one call at a time, the control staffs had to deal with all the 999, GP's calls and hospital calls. Along with all the radio traffic coming in from crews asking for all kinds of information or asking for information to be passed on to hospitals, it is a non stop environment. It is a very demanding and very responsible part of the ambulance service.

All of the control room staff have to put up with as much abuse as road staff do from the public. Whilst the abuse is over the phone it is still unwarranted. Strangely, but thankfully the service does not suffer as many malicious 999 calls as the fire service or the police. They are the back bone of the service,it is more responsible in achieving the ORCON standard (Operational Research Consultancy) than all the rest of the managers. The control manager has to give a reason on every call that misses this standard. It is a fast and dynamic place in which to work, I have done it and it was not for me, my rear end doesn't like sitting down for too long. As my granddad said, when my son Andrew was born, with his right ear missing.

'He couldn't even wait to finish that job off!'

It is a multi tasking environment and far more suitable to be run by females who have this capability than us mere males (What a Sexist remark that's an official warning)

The other thing that makes me smile is listening to the many objections made by the fire service in having regional fire controls. Beds and Herts, fire service when I left were dealing with combined calls of 60 calls a day! So who says that these new fire regional centres will not be able to cope?

During the ambulance dispute when the crews withdrew their labour from November to March, I along with all the other officers in the service attended as many calls as deemed necessary for patient's welfare. I had to attend the Hertfordshire police HQ where we had arranged for calls to be sent, after they had been called into our control room. It was my job to take the phone calls from our ambulance control room, I would then sort out what army or police vehicle was nearby to attend the incident. This was handed over to a policeman to mobilise the vehicle. If they needed advice or help on a medical nature I then could speak to them direct or have an ambulance officer sent on.

I seemed once again to be the unlucky person, a call had come into ambulance control of a child having an asthma attack, it was passed on to me as an officer had been dispatched but was some distance away. I directed a police vehicle to be sent to the address, but for some unknown reason it took a good thirty minutes to arrive. The child was taken into hospital and that was that I thought. About two hours later a woman had managed to gain access to the police HQ, also gained access into the room. She burst in, shouting abuse at us, singling out me as I was in ambulance makings, saying that her child could have died because of the length of time we had taken to fetch her child and then into hospital. She was taken out of the room by the police and duly dealt with, but in a sympathetic manner though.

The next time it was my turn to work in the police room, I walked into the entrance and was greeted by several armed police guarding the door! Having checked me out to see if I was the person I said I was they let me in. Obviously the first thing I asked the police what was all the security was about? Well they said that it all started the other week when an RTA happened on the A505 between Baldock and Royston. The police had arrived prior to the army ambulance, and just before that had arrived, a car had failed to slow down at the accident and ran into a policeman and killed him. The Army NCO who arrived and dealt with the scene was distressed by the whole situation and had a big argument with his Major over it. The NCO went AWOL (absent without leave) the next they heard about the NCO was that he had been out of the country but had got back in at Dover, and was apparently armed. It was thought he might come to the police headquarters to seek his Army Major. A large man hunt was on to find the NCO, and the Army Major was given police protection. The NCO was later arrested and handed over to the Military Police.

If an ambulance went into an Accident & Emergency department with a patient the crews should become available to deal with another call within twenty minutes. But that was becoming more of an issue with a reduction in staff at the A&E dept. to hand the patient over to. The lack of beds to place the patient on, could lead up to an hour to offload a patient from an ambulance. This had serious implications because as more ambulances went into A&E departments the more ambulances were sitting there unable to unload their patient. This meant that ambulances had to attend incidents coming in from other areas, to plug the holes left by those loaded ambulances waiting to discharge their patient at the hospitals. This causes complications for control and leads to some heated exchanges between the control and the hospital. The senior Nurse would shout at the manager in control to stop bringing patients into their hospital! No I never fathomed that one out either, even when I went to see the A&E sister about this remark, she just shouted at me hoping by doing this we would give in to her demand. But armed with Department of Health Circular which stated you cannot close an A&E unit because you are understaffed or have an influx of patients, it can only be closed if you have no doctors to operate the unit and this must only come from the senior manager on duty at the time, even if it meant the Chief Executive of the hospital using a phone!. As you can imagine this went down like a lead balloon, and so did she.

Along with my director we obtained ambulance trolleys, so the patient could be left at the A&E department, and we could take the empty trolleys and carry on with further calls. Even though this was agreed with A&E consultant the nursing staff then started heated arguments with the ambulance crews for so called "Just Dumping" patients with no care. It was not our problem to look after other health service funding issues, as we had our own.

Another big headache for my operational and control managers and me, to deal with was meal breaks. This got more difficult to manage when the crews changed from eight hour shifts to twelve hour shifts, with the ever increasing work load and some times with a small resource to deal with it. Staff would come on duty between 06.00hrs and 0700 and work a twelve hour shift, the majority of doctors calls started to come in from about 11,30hrs onwards when they had finished their morning surgery and went on their home visits. They would arrange admissions to either the local hospital or to a specialist hospital further away, causing more problems. As the local hospital doctors were also arranging for some of their patients to go on to a specialist hospital. So pressure was placed on crews to work through their lunch break between 1100/1400hrs and they would get £3.50 for the privilege, but as crews said they could not eat money but preferred to have food. If the ambulance needed filling up with fuel it can't just carry on with nothing in the tank, neither can we. It was an issue that could not be easily resolved without more resources, or patients suffering a longer wait for an ambulance. Controllers work really hard to get crews their lunch break, often themselves going without their allotted breaks.

They would be criticised by road staff for not doing their job properly (99.9% the road staff were wrong). But you must remember no one likes getting told what they have to do, even though it's their job to work!

As I have said when the ambulance service became a NHS Trust everything was money led. And I was present at several meetings with our paymaster as this was being set up. Basically, parts of Beds & Herts. were split into areas, for running the hospitals, stores and all other NHS related budgets.

When it came to discussing who was going to pay for what patients I asked

'Who was going to pay for people going into a Hospice'

Stunned silence, then 'What do you mean' They asked,

So I said again

'Who is going to pay for patients needing to go into a hospice for terminal care'

To be honest with you they looked at me with blank expressions as if I had come from Mars, I even had to look behind me to see if they were looking at something on the wall. It took about ten minutes of them talking amongst themselves to work out a solution.

'Well how many patients are we talking about and what area is taking in the most Patients'

Now I know I joined the ambulance service to look after patients but maybe I needed to change my attitude to this new way of thinking Money was now God.

Can we afford it, if not leave the patient where they were I was saying to myself. Was I becoming a Dinosaur? That thought was in my head for a millie second, and. I replied

'Well if it's two a week two a month or two a year, does it really matter as these patients were not going there to recover they were going there to die with some help and dignity'

Clearing of throats all round and without further discussing it was passed that we could move these patients with the proviso, that they would be marked as special movement on the return forms. It still makes my blood boil as I think about it now.

Another day another meeting with same people, there had been a lot of newspaper reports that we were not achieving our targets of getting an ambulance to some of the out lying villages, Orcon standard being, within 19minutes and 59seconds. Having discussed this issue for some time, the senior member said

'Well if they chose to live in these places, they have to put up with the consequences'

I replied 'That they pay the same taxes and health taxes as everybody else, haven't these people got a case'

This went down like a horse shit sandwich. The reply was eye contact and it was utter contempt! During a coffee break I just happened to say out loud as I was so pissed off,

'It appears to be the government's intention to hope more people die before their retirement so they don't have to pay them a pension'

No comment as they backed off me like I was a leper.

More meetings with the Police Service, the Fire service, Health Authority and the County Emergency Planning Committee. We had to make and submit contingency plans in the case of major incidents. These were very varied. After the disaster at Hillsborough where Liverpool were playing in the semi final of the football cup against Nottingham Forest, in which 97 Liverpool football fans lost there lives.

A committee was set up by the government to see what improvements could be put into place to make football grounds a safer place to go to. This was carried out by Lord Justice Taylor. His report which became known as the Taylor report enforced all football clubs through out England to have a standard procedure of safety. This affected the two football professional football clubs in our area, Watford F.C. and Luton F.C., they had to have a safety committee, and to have an NHS Ambulance in attendance with crowds over 6000. I sat on the safety committee for Watford F.C., and having been a Watford supporter since I was born in Watford, it came as no hardship to me. This also involved me being the ambulance officer in charge at all home games. Much to the disgust of my son, I sometimes had to attend the "Sworn Enemy" as my son will tell you "Luton town football club ground".

I also had to sit on the safety committee for Knebworth Park near Stevenage where the group Oasis were going to have at that time, the biggest live audience attending a concert. This also involved me being the senior Ambulance officer in charge. The concert was great success and I thoroughly enjoyed those two nights and the music. Unfortunately! Some of my officers and staff had to work quite hard under some testing conditions.

We had several major sites that needed separate emergency contingency plans in place, Luton airport for one. We held an annual exercise along with Police and Fire Service as well as airport staff to make sure we could deal with real thing if it ever happened. This was to insure that all the services worked together.

It also made sure the airport met the standards to have for its Civil Aviation licence to be renewed.

We also had two prisons Bovingdon and Bedford in our area. Not only having to concern ourselves with any kind of major incident within the prison, but to insure all staff were aware, of moving any prisoner to hospital after an assault or an illness. As we were told by the prison Governor this was the most likely time a prisoner would try to escape.

Buncefield at Hemel Hempstead housed a large petroleum site. These blew up in 2005 and this was the biggest fire in Europe since WW11. Luckily only three people were slightly injured. If this had happened on a week day the estimated number of dead could have been in excess of 300 and over 4000 injured. The fire service exercised here more than us, because we knew it would be their problem, and also for the police with M1 Motorway running along side this site.

One night I was rung up at home about 2300 hrs by a police inspector from Hemel Hempstead warning me of a report that had come their way of a possibility of an attack by the IRA on Buncefield. The Intelligence suggested that a vehicle would stop on the hard shoulder of the motorway and fire off mortar bombs onto the petroleum site at Buncefield, and did I have a plan? Well the first thing I said was,

'As I lived in Hertford I was alright Jack! I'll be over when the explosion is over and see what I could do'

Well I don't know if he thought I was serious or not and said.

'Oh, ah well, don't you have any plan'

I reassured him that he should know we have contingency plans, but more importantly, what were the police doing about this problem? He said that

'That's what he was trying to sort out'

I wished him well and my closing remark to him was,

'Try and find a tin helmet for your self.'

He struggled to laugh at my remark. As I always said to people, if you can't take a joke you shouldn't have joined!

With all my dealings with the police service up to the level of Assistant Chief Constable I got the reputation that before my arrival at an incident the scene was a disaster, on my arrival it turned into a bloody catastrophe! It was a great working relationship!

With my opening on ambulance staffs not mentioned enough for some of the outstanding work they do. I would like to mention some of outstanding work of a few of them that I had the privilege to work with.

Dave an ambulance man from our station was awarded the Royal Humane Society medal for outstanding courage. Along with his colleague Gerry he attended a call to a boy drowning in a lake. On their arrival they were told the location where the child was last seen in the water. Without hesitation Dave stripped off and jumped straight into the lake and swam down as far as he could. Even though being unsuccessful on locating the child on numerous dives, he carried on until he was overcome with exhaustion.

The police had to call an under water specialist team to recover the little boy. That took time to arrange, so Dave and Gerry were released. The child was later recovered, and the police said that the child had got tangled in thick weeds deep down just off from where Dave had been diving. The police incident officer said that Dave was lucky not to have been caught up in this vegetation himself. They recommended he should be awarded for his bravery for the following reasons. He took upon himself to enter the water with out any thought for his own safety hoping to rescue the child.

Strangle enough he did not receive a Chief Officers commendation, but none the less, all of us were all extremely pleased that he received this award.

It was now the turn of Gerry to receive a Chief Officers commendation, which we all believed were locked away in Fort Knox because they were as rare as Hens teeth.

His commendation came about following an RTA on the M 1, junction six with the M25. A lorry had overturned, trapping the driver in his cab. Gerry managed to climb into the cab to give support and medical aid to the driver, while efforts were made by the Fire Service to extricate him. For some unknown reason we could not locate a doctor, to give any pain killing drugs or other medical help. Gerry was in the cab, with the driver for nearly three hours, during which time the patient went through six cylinders of Entonox and one large F size cylinders of oxygen.

Once the driver was released from his cab Gerry had to be supported out of the cab as well, because he had got himself into such a position that he had been unable to move whilst he was supporting the driver during this rescue. Following that rescue he had to have two days off sick, because he had lost the use of an arm and severe cramp in his legs.

The whole of St Albans station staff volunteered for extra work, after a serious coach crash in France, involving children from two schools from St.Albans area. Several children had been killed and over twenty five had been injured and ten seriously, as well as their teachers. One member of my staff came to ask if, when the children are repatriated back to England could we voluntary take these children either, on to their home addresses or to the hospitals they were allocated to. It appeared that the children were being flown back to British Aerospace at Hatfield. The reason for this was a number of the children's parents worked at the British Aerospace site, at Hatfield so B.A.C. were sending their own planes to France to collect the less seriously injured with their parents.

We approached the Chief Ambulance Officer who agreed to this request without hesitation. It was my task to coordinate the staff and get volunteers, and without any hesitation all staff put their names forward, including the P T S. When the first planes arrived in the evening we managed to take children, parents and luggage to either their homes or hospital.

Over the next three days the more seriously injured children were flown home in air ambulance with medical staff. These children had to be taken to specialist hospitals one going as far as Warwickshire

During that three day period I only had about six hours sleep. But I was very proud of every member of my staff who contributed to getting these children and worried parents to their destinations without further trauma being added to their already horrific experience.

At a Civic reception held in the Town Hall in St. Albans one schools Head Masters said in his speech how wonderful the ambulance staff had treated the children on their arrival back in the UK. It had saved all the worry and the logistics of how the children were going to get their destinations.

More heroics and commendations were given to, two members of staff. I was called to a house explosion early one morning caused by gas, and on my arrival I was astounded to find just one large pile of rubble which once was a house, it was completely devastated. The fire brigade had set to work to rescue three people who were trapped in this house, along side them was the crew of one ambulance, Jan and Andy. They had somehow got into this completely wrecked house to carry out aid to the injured occupants. After an hour one adult was released along with one of her daughters, the other daughter would remain trapped for a further three hours. Jan and Andy and Jan remained inside the house whilst the fire service carried out the rescue. All three patients had a miraculous escape and only received minor injuries.

My director was also on scene with me which was unusual, and we agreed that this crew should receive an award for their bravery.

We were all pleased that a special occasion was set up for this. The Lord Lieutenant of Bedfordshire, Sam Whitbread presented them with a special award for bravery.

The citation read that they had risked life and limb staying with their trapped patient in the upturned roof of a house after a gas explosion in Hemel Hempstead. Gas was still pumping out whilst they stayed helping to clear the rubble from around the patient and just prior to getting the patient out of the rubble the gable end was starting to fall in on them.

Bob Cass Director of Operations went on to say that they had showed great courage,   and it is with great pride that we make this award.

A little while latter the BBC, did a reconstruction for their 999 series.

One of the strange things that has happened over-time is the way more and more staff are being abused verbally as well as physically by the general public when they are trying to deal with patients. When I joined the service ambulance staff and nurses were treated with respect even by drunks but now the young people of today don't give a shit about people, trying to help them or about anything else I suppose. I might be generalising here, but on the whole when called to an incident involving youngster who have more than share of a sherbet they are abusive to us, nursing staff and the police and that's even when they are trying to help someone .

One can expect the genuinely ill patients like diabetics and patients with head injuries, who through no fault of their own can be aggressive and abusive, but some people just like to have a go at any body in a uniform.

I had to attend 18 members of my staff who had to make statements to the police after being assaulted 2 being threatened by a man with knife. Equipment being take and stolen off ambulances, on ten occasions. Ambulances being driven off stolen "For a joy ride", but normally dumped with in a mile or so, some with serious damage. Criminal damage caused, either to the interior, exterior of the ambulance. Stations broken into and items stolen.

As with any organization that employs a large number of staff there has to be a bad apple. One day I had a phone call from a patient's relative who said. that her mothers wedding ring was missing, after a crew had picked her up and taken her into hospital, and wondered if it had been handed in. I said I would make some inquires and come back to her which I did the following day. Having identified the crew I rang them at home to see if they remembered the patient. Having ascertained that they didn't have the ring or knowledge of it, I rang the daughter and said that I had drawn a blank, and all I could suggest, if she was not satisfied she should report it to the police, who could investigate far better than we could. We always told the complainant of lost property to call the police if they were not satisfied with our explanation.

Now before I go on with this story I must say two things. I have had an accusation made about me and my colleague after dealing with an RTA, on the M1.A male person lost a wedding ring after being run over several times by cars and killed. Apart from the obvious damage done to the body of this man, his wife was insistent that he wore an expensive wedding ring always. On arrival at hospital we had the male certified dead, by the casualty doctor. We asked him if he would accompany us into the mortuary. Our reason for doing this, we explained to him was so that he could witness us placing the body in the fridge without touching any of his clothing or removing any belongings. As we did so we pointed out that there was no wrist watch or rings even though this man was black there were marks where a watch and a ring might have been worn, the doctor said he agreed with us and we all left the mortuary together.

Imagine my surprise a week later, when my colleague and I were told by our station officer to go the police station and make a statement, about our fatal accident on the M1 involving missing property. Off we went thinking it wasn't going to be a problem so we thought, independently made a statement saying what we had done and how we got the casualty doctor involved, and off we went. Two days later we were both summoned back to the police station and once again in separate rooms we were asked to go through our story again and I repeated what I said before.

I asked 'Hadn't the doctor verified what we had said?

To my gut wrenching horror the policeman said 'No he had not'

The blood drained from me as I knew I was telling the truth. But how was I going to prove it, then I suddenly remembered that I as alighted from the ambulance I was blinded by a flash from a camera, it was the local Evening Echo Newspaper photographer, who was taking pictures of the accident. I told the policeman who was taking my statement about this and that the newspaper might have a photograph of the body before we had arrived, and it might just show that there was no ring on this mans hand.

Much to mine and my colleague's relief, the police contacted us a week later to say the photographs had shown that the man had not been wearing a ring prior to our arrival. To be honest I felt sick for those two to three weeks being under suspicion and even sicker after being told I was innocent.

I can only remember on one occasion of an ambulance man being prosecuted for stealing from a patient during my years in the service.

Beds police approached my station officer and me, that they were investigating reports that suggested various items were going missing after an ambulance was called to patient's houses. They supplied us with the addresses and asked if we could see if it was one particular crew that was involved in all these calls.

After some paper work the station officer came up with one person's name which the police seemed to like! They asked us if we would be prepared to do a fake removal of a patient and they would then see if anything went missing from the address using this crew. I said I would run it past my Director but I knew he would not object and he didn't.

The police came up with an address to operate the fake removal from with the help of a retired policewoman who was going to be the patient needing to go into hospital.

We had to inform the senior manager of the local Accident and Emergency department and also the control manager what we were about to do. All this was carried out with only these five people knowing what was going to happen.

The appointed day came with the police putting several objects in drawers and lying around in the house, plus they had all these items covered by CCTV.

The patient was picked up by the appointed crew and taken into hospital. We waited to be informed by the police, to see if any items had been removed. A policeman was in my office to inform me if we needed to have this crew called back to our station where they would be arrested. The call came from the police at the patient's house confirming that items had been taken by one crew member. The crew took the patient into the hospital and handed her over to the A&E staff. As the crew called control to inform them that they were available to carry out another job, control informed them return to their station. Immediately on their return both crew members were arrested by the police, and taken to the police station in two separate cars.

The unfortunate side of this was, that one crew member was completely innocent and had no knowledge of what his colleague had been up to. He went off sick for some weeks with the shock of being arrested.

When the ambulance man went to court he was only given community service and probation. We were all bitterly disappointed at this very lenient sentence because we believe that the sentence should have been prison at least, he was in a position of trust and he had betrayed that trust to the patient, his work colleagues, and to all ambulance men and women.

For some time I had been very concerned over some injuries involving children. Having taken on the Herts County Council over injuries, that had acured whilst children were in school. I was also concerned that children had been abused, but we had not picked that up, either because we were not sharp enough or we had been totally misled.

For some unknown and crazy reason all managers had to go to Luton University to set for a management certificate, having down the job for years we all had to prove we knew what we were doing! Just more waste of money

So when Tony had to go, I gave him his assignment to have a Child Protection policy for the service. He had to liaise with the two police child protection units in Beds & Herts. Doctors who had the knowledge on how some injuries could be masked.

He came up with a very good system that had to be brought to every front line ambulance staff as well as officers and control room staff. All the training was carried out by him with talks given by doctors who gave up their time to train us. This taught us what signs to look for, on entering a house, and the behaviour of some parents on the way they answered any questions. This took nothing away from informing the hospital who had their own system for reporting abuse. This was a back up system that was reported to an officer and any suspicion was passed on to the police for them if necessary, to deal with. We had no way, if what we had reported to the police was of use or not, as it was considered confidential by the agencies.

In 1998, I along with nine other of my colleagues, were sent off to America to learn how the Ambulance service operates. It was not a Jolly, we spent most of the time in the class room. We were being shown how we would meet the increase number of calls and to get to the scene much quicker. We went to Kansas City and then to Saginaw Michigan. We went out on the ambulances to see how the crews worked.

The ambulances are governed to 65mph and have a black box to insure that it was kept to. If any interventions of drugs were needed for a patient, permission had to be gained from the receiving hospital. Most calls that needed an ambulance had the attendance of the fire service!

We had gone all that way to be shown that!

When the ambulance returned to base, they had a person who checked the ambulance for stock and it cleaned as well.

All this was already been introduced in Staffordshire ambulance service, called Stockers and Washers. The other big feature in the USA was that they had standby points, and as an ambulance was called away from that standby point another one took its place. Once again this was already in use in Staffordshire.

We were treated very well by everybody that we came across, and we visited ambulance stations, police stations and hospitals but to be honest the Americans could learn more from us. Whilst they have the money to throw at things and the resources but on this occasion we do it better.

CHAPTER 10:
Critical Incident Debriefing

Unfortunately some staff got to some point in their career where they could not cope with either coming on duty, having periods of time off sick with some spurious reason, or acting in a strange manner. This had troubled me for some time because it appeared to me, little was being done to address these staff issues. I would, if identified by me or the station officers, sit down with the member of staff and talk through the issues that might be troubling them.

Over the years, I have been able to cope with what I seen and dealt with. I have been able to deflect some of these incidents by black humour, talking things over with my colleagues. I never got hardened to jobs, because that seems heartless or cold. But certain calls still remain with me, because these patients have touched me in some way as I have touched them. I love dealing with people which has help me, I believe in copping with situations.

Unfortunately it came to a head to one L/a in Berkhampstead. I was called to a RTA. Control had a call for extra ambulance but no reason was given or a sitrep given. When I arrived at the scene it appeared that every bit of equipment had been removed from the back of the first ambulance on the scene, all the equipment was strewn all over the road it look as if the ambulance had been ransacked. Having ensured that the scene was cleared of all patients by first ambulance, and the following two ambulances, I ask control to send me crew in an unequipped ambulance so that I could clear the road of all the equipment.

I then asked the police if they could help me by telling me what had happened here. They said that when they arrived, they found one ambulance man had taken all the kit out of the ambulance and thrown it about. They were very perplex as to what had gone on, but as I had arrived they thought someone was worried about this strange happing and I would sort out problem.

I asked control to return the crew to me at Hemel station that had caused this problem. I took the L/a who was in charge into the office to ask what had gone on at the RTA. But I noticed straight away, as soon as he sat down he was rocking backwards and forwards in the chair and was in no fit state to talk to me. He had in my opinion had a "Breakdown", he was unfortunately a complete mess. He was very unwell and needed to go home. It was no use taking him to the hospital as they were not in a position to help him. I got his colleague to take him home, and to ensure that his wife called his doctor in the morning. Please tell her the station officer will visit them in the morning to see what help we could be. When his colleague came back to the station I asked what had gone on at the accident. He said that the L/a, had been acting strange when he came on duty and when they got the call to the RTA he just appeared to lose it and could not cope with the situation.

In the morning the station officer (Jean) went to the L/As home to see how he was. Jean spoke to his wife who told her that really she was not surprised when he came home. He had been unable to cope with the job for some time. Jean asked if he had sought any help from his GP or informed anybody at the station, she said that he had not. Jean asked her to call his GP and keep her updated as to his progress and hope when he was feeling better we could come and see him.

After about six weeks we did see him again and to be honest I was not happy with the GPs response, it appeared all he had done was put him, on tranquilisers and told him to rest.

After a long chat with him to try and see how this "Breakdown" had come about. He told me, that that the responsibility of the running the station, dealing with new staff, and having dealt with several serious incidents he had, had enough. He talked about going on to work on trains, which had always been his passion. We told him to take as much time off as he wanted, and come and see us when he felt he could talk more. We also told him to go back to his GP to see if he could get any more help, in the way of counselling. Unfortunately he was unable to make a successful return to the ambulance service. He went to work on the railways, which I was very pleased to hear sometime later that he was doing very well.

Christmas I was woken by a phone call from control and the manager told me '(name) has arrested at Luton ambulance station'.

I had travelled four miles when an update came from control manager telling me the ambulance woman was on route by ambulance to Luton and Dunstable A&E,

Suspended breathing! This threw me completely, because I thought the ambulance woman had been arrested by the police, I asked control for more information on what was going on. The manager, who I believe had a problem with me as she rarely spoke to me at the best of times, then informed me that the ambulance woman had been found hanging in a cupboard on the station by her other crew colleagues. I asked her to inform the station manager of the situation and tell him to attend the station immediately.

I went to the hospital to see how the member of staff was but unfortunately she had been declared dead by the A&E doctor prior to my arrival. This was an unprecedented incident and all of us who dealt with it were all completely shocked. I informed the Chief Executive and my Director about the incident, they both turned out from their homes immediately. They came and gave support to the members of staff on the station, who had all worked extremely hard to resuscitate her. The staffs on the station were very grateful that the Chief had turned out.

It appeared that this ambulance woman had come on duty and then disappeared, when a call came in, her crew member couldn't find her. All the other staff started looking for her and found her hanging in a cupboard.

The crews were taken off call whilst the police tried to piece together what happened. The station officer and my self went to see the mother of the ambulance woman and to take her and other members of the family to the hospital and gave them as much support as we could.

This ambulance woman had been seen both by me and her station officer on several occasions to see if she had any problems. We felt that she never interacted with other members of staff. Whenever she was on station she would go into the meeting room and write, what she said was going to be a novel which she hoped would be published and she was happy doing her work. From the L/a, crews, station manger and myself we would try and talk to her and cajole her into being more sociable but without much success. We also knew of an ambulance man who was similar to her on another station and he liked his own company.

There were other members of staff that if the right kind of support or help could have been provided I am sure would have stayed in the service. Some called it the bell syndrome where as soon as the phone rang they would felt physically sick. Why these members of staff had got to a situation where they would struggle to cope with, what they might face I don't know. But if only they would or could talk to other members of staff their managers or even their GP's I am sure that some of their issues would have been resolved. But staff thought that we, the "Management" would not take any notice or worse still try to have them dismissed from the service. I can assure you that no members of my management team or me ever thought of this. These ambulance men and woman had been highly trained by us, and we didn't want to lose any of them, as all members of staff were doing excellent work.

So imagine my delight when one day I went to a HESMIC (Hertfordshire Emergency Services Major Incident Committee) seminar. These seminars are held annually, and bring all different services together who have dealt with a Major incident in their area during the previous year. They pass on their experiences, what they learnt from it, and any mistakes they made, so we could learn from the experience.

One of the speakers was a former senior police officer who was a lecturer at Bramfield Police Collage. Andy talked on the duty of care we owe our staff. And he had devised a system called Critical Incident Debriefing within the Metropolitan police.

He was trying to make us appreciate that some of our staff would suffer from post traumatic stress syndrome (P T S D). As his talk went on, certain things stuck in mind that I had heard through out my career such as 'If they don't like the heat then you should get out of the kitchen'

'If you don't like it you know what you can do'

These sound bites, statements were well past their sell by date and could be used in an industrial tribunal against the employer

He likens it to over loading a lorry, you can only put on a certain amount of tonnage, or otherwise you overload it, the chassis will break.

'Let's face it' he went on

'We look after our equipment better than our staff, we test it every day we send vehicles into workshops to be serviced every 6000 miles, a major service every twelve thousand miles, what do we do our with staff? We give them demands like oh can you just do this other job while you are near by! It won't take you long'

He went onto say 'That nobody will own up to being off with stress they would rather   say, I have flu, diarrhoea, or a cold.'

He was absolutely right we didn't look after the staff even though we had an occupational health department. It seemed there only concern, if you had been off sick for some length of time, they would tell you when you could comeback to work and how this would be done.

He had trained a core of serving police officers to be Critical Incident Debriefers (CID). These trained staff would intervene in a certain incident that serving police officers had identified as a traumatic event that could cause stress to the officers who had dealt with situation. This is exactly what we needed, a system that could help our staff and hopefully stop the likes of the ambulance woman hanging herself, or staff feeling, before they came on duty worrying themselves sick, or hitting the bottle. Because they were worried as how they were going to cope, with what might happen, in the coming hours, whilst they were on duty.

I approached my director Bob who said in principle he liked the idea, and to go and make a case to sell it to the management board to see if they would fund it. This was duly done and I set about implementing the system.

Andy trained fourteen of us to become Critical Incident Debriefers including my Director Bob Cass and another manager Dave Guy and me, the rest being road staff and a control officer.

CID is not counselling, it is a form of structured psychological debriefing conducted in small groups. It is a direct action-oriented crisis intervention process designed to prevent or mitigate traumatic stress. It was originally designed to reduce stress in emergency service personnel after extremely traumatic experiences.

There are no notes taken during or after a debriefing session and it is extremely confidential to all the people that taking part in the session

The debriefing has three phases. The structure allows participants in the group to discuss their traumatic incident in a controlled manner which does not leave them feeling out of control of themselves. The debriefing process uses certain techniques common to counselling, but is not counselling or psychotherapy nor a substitute for either. One of the main components which make debriefing different is the fact that it deals with the immediacy of the situation, and that a substantial portion of the debriefing process is dedicated to enabling participants to understand the process, and nature of their stress reactions. Individual and group stress survival techniques to manage traumatic stress are also explored.

It is important that the Debriefers have an expertise in dealing with and understanding the special needs of the staff involved. If this is not the case, the ability of the debriefing team to achieve the primary goals of debriefing will be severely jeopardised.

During the course of debriefing you bring in the three key words

<u>Facts</u> > Thoughts	Impressions		Expectations	Decisions
<u>Feelings</u> > Helplessness	Frustration	Guilt		Anger
<u>Future</u> > Coping	Communication		Mobilising support	
	Understanding reactions	Additional help	Sharing	

Time course of post-traumatic stress reactions

The course was spread over three days and the group were extremely excited to try out their new skills. We first had to draw up of a list of what we considered to be a CID intervention. Whilst the list we drew up was not a definitive list, we gave what we considered to be the main head line calls. Long Entrapments that lead to the death whilst treating the patient, children's deaths, death of a work colleague, assault on members of staff, being involved in an Rta, anything out of the ordinary from the crew perception that needed an intervention. These also involved members of the control room who, in their way were dealing with the call and all subsequent calls that came from the road staff.

We always ended up by informing the staff that they might experience flash backs about their incident or even dreams. This was a normal reaction but these should start to diminish after thirty days. If this was not the case we could offer more help to them.

Whilst it got off to a slow start with the staff because of some scepticism, confidence soon grew as more and more road staff took part in being debriefed. We believed in the first year of our interventions that sickness dropped by at least 5%.

What pleased me even more, is when the staff started to come forward not only to say they wanted to be debriefed over an incident that we had been unaware of, but a small number of staff wanted to be counselled in the conventional means, which meant we retained more staff and they came back to work better equipped to carry on.

Andy asked Dave and I to help train other Health professionals and police officers around the country with CID. This for me was one of the best things that happened to the service for some years, all because I was lucky enough to attend a seminar.

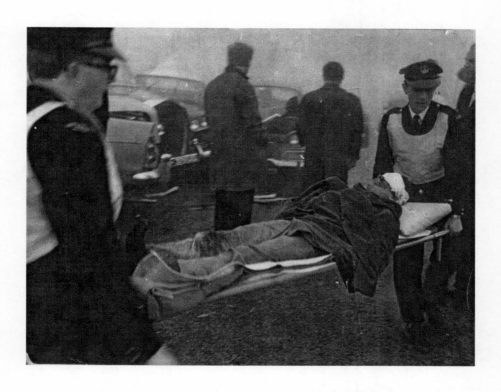

M1 Multiple accident involving the Aston Martin etc.

Copyright Echo & Post

Bank raid Hemel Hempstead Minus my cap again

Copyright Echo & Post

Swiss Air Ambulance bringing one of the seriously injured
children back from the coach crash in France

Copyright Hert Advertiser

Illustrates M1 with no crash barrier

Copyright Echo & Post

Lorry off the A10 viaduct

Taken by my stepson Gary Saban

Crews working in the severe storm without pay

Copyright Gary Saban

Car into tree which caused the severe injuries to the patient's testicles

Copyright Gary Saban

*M25 the remains of a lorry cab after it
crossed over the Armco barrier*

Copyright Author

The train crash at Watford

Copyright Author

My wife and I outside Buckingham Palace

Copyright Author

CHAPTER 11:
Sudden Illness

Sudden illness is the highest amount of emergency calls that all ambulance services deal with. These can be calls for heart attacks, strokes, asthma, diabetics and fits, Illnesses that come on suddenly and anything else the general public make up for us to attend. It's now the norm for calls from alcohol abuse after the pub and clubs have closed down for the night. These are not sudden illnesses but no one else knows what to do about them, so they call an ambulance to attend. We take them to the Accident & Emergency department so the staff there have to put up with abuse and fights from these mindless people. The police have to deal with all these problems as well, and their resources get tied up dealing with this social problem costing millions every year when this money could be put to much better use.

When I first joined the service none of the following calls gave us a problem, abuse, drink and drugs, but as more young people got money in their pockets, it became a growing problem. A time bomb in the making as doctors spell out the mental health issues that will arise from taking drugs. Alcohol is causing harm, not only in physical harm, but in fights and premature deaths.

GPs have given up, giving a night service to their patients. I have a friend who was my village GP when it was his turn to be on call at night, he never went to bed, but just rested in his Parker chair. That went for great majority of country GP's. With the population becoming more migratory, not signing on with doctors, either people would call for an ambulance, or just turn up at the hospitals for the least little thing.

As well as the Mental Hospitals I have mentioned we had in our area, hospitals that would now be called people with special needs. 'Cell Barnes and Harperbury Hospital' Gerry was called to Cell Barnes hospital to a male person taken seriously ill. Apparently this person would lie in bed all day, and spin a book on his finger and in the next bed to him another male person would do exactly the same but spin it in the opposite direction. Having conveyed him to St.Albans hospital, a further call came in to convey the remaining book spinner. He went into serious decline as though he was pining for his book spinning mate. We got this call and duly took him into St.Albans but on our arrival we heard the other patient had just died. Our poor patient although not knowing this, died a few hours later.

No ambulance person likes hearing the following, either over the phone or the radio, 'Proceed to a home where it believed to be a baby Purple (dead)'. Having done too many of these, it really hurts everyone involved in these incidents. Several stand out in my memory. Sunday morning we were called to a baby dumped on the door step in St. Albans. We discovered a dead baby wrapped, in a shopping bag, dumped on a doorstep in a shop doorway! How any one can dump a baby without making a phone call or informing someone I do not know? They must under severe pressure to do the right thing but unable to cope with the situation.

We were met by a mum in the front garden of her very large house holding her baby in her arms, we saw straight away the baby was purple but we started mouth to mouth. I asked what had happened.

'He (the baby) had been in his pram all morning I just went to feed him and found him like this'

I was appalled on hearing this, because it had been below freezing all morning and whilst there was bright sun, her front garden was facing north with no sunlight. On arrival at the hospital the doctors worked for some time on the baby but called the death after about thirty minutes. I informed the police of our findings and what the mother had told us and I was willing to attend a coroner's court if needed. I felt this baby's death could have been prevented and I believed this baby had been neglected by the mother. I heard no more about this sad case, perhaps I was being too harsh on her.

The more I go in writing this book, Sunday's calls seem to figure quite prominently. Usually its quiet and we would give the ambulances a good clean. The bells alert us and the fire brigade to a house, child collapsed in the bathroom mother unable to gain access. Off we went, racing the fire appliance to the scene, we all entered the house and the mother explained to us that she didn't think he had been over come by the gas water heater, but was not sure. The door was kicked in by a fireman size 10 boots! There was a boy of 15 years lying in the bath up to his waist in water, unconscious.

We carried him down the stairs and put him into our ambulance, we did a quick check on him and rushed him off to the casualty department. As we were leaving the address the fire service were calling the gas board to come and check the water heater in case it was a gas leak.

We were entering the hospital when the boy came round and said

'What's happing to me'

I told him he was going to be ok and asked him if he remember any thing about today.

'No'

I asked him if he had had a late night or been busy doing anything this weekend, such as sport.

'No' again he replied

Then he said rather sheepishly.

'Well I started wanking for the first time on Friday night; I liked it so much I haven't stopped, I have been doing it every half hour!'

Just then my mate opened the doors of the ambulance, I was glad he did because, I had to jump out and rushed straight into the casualty department, to find the sister as I was having a fit of the giggles at this boy's honesty. The Sister who was Swedish thought it was great and said it was no wonder he had collapse. We came out to the ambulance to help the boy into her department telling him he was going to be fine.

My mate then asked me what the hell was going on. So I told him and he couldn't stop laughing, but we had to stop pretty quickly, because mum and dad had now turned up in their car and we couldn't be seen laughing.

A similar call given to me one night I was dispatched to a house in the Luton area. To attend a female believed to be deceased at her home address, the nearest ambulance was some twenty minutes away. Control asked if I would assess the situation, to see if an ambulance was needed or render aid until it arrived. At the house I was ushered in by a very anxious young male who rushed me upstairs saying it was his girlfriend who had died whilst they were having sex! He said again that she just appeared to die on him! He had not done mouth to mouth! As I put my defibrillator down I noticed she was still breathing. So I touched her arm and asked her if she could hear me there was a slight stir so I pinched her ear lob and spoke to her again she opened her eyes and jumped up saying 'What's going on'

I told her what her boyfriend had told me, as by now he had just slumped to the floor crying. All she could think of was that she must have fallen asleep because she had a hard day! That brought a smile to face I can tell you, and I am not going to tell you what else I was thinking either. I asked all the usual questions, are you on any medication, have you been ill recently, does this happen often that you suddenly fall asleep. She said no all these questions. So I could only come to the same conclusion as her. As for boyfriend, well I think he was very embarrassed on a number of issues, so I left them to it, as I went merrily home thinking!

Marks & Spencer's in St Albans a male collapsed. his legs have gone! We strode into the store to be met by the patient's wife, informing us his artificial leg had broken. It appeared that the screws that held the knee joint on his artificial leg had loosened and falling out with no trace. Strictly speaking it was not a casualty issue but we said we would take him and see if one of the technicians could help out. So without thinking I picked up the leg to take it back to the ambulance and to get our carry chair so that we could wheel him back to the ambulance. As I walked out of the store two ladies who had stood outside to have a nose at what was going on, saw me with leg and promptly fainted!

Promptly putting the leg down to attend to these two ladies, when someone else pushed their way through the crowed to have a nose, and saw the ladies plus the leg on the floor, she went down like a sack of potatoes too. My colleague who thought I was taking longer than I should to get the chair, decided he would come out to find me, he was promptly met with me up to my eyes in fallen women. 'Bloody hell Gordon I've got to hand it to you, as I have always said, you have a strange effect on women'

'Thanks' I said

And off he went to call for another ambulance. We managed to bring these ladies round. None of the ladies wanted to go hospital for a check up, and when I told them why I was carrying the leg, they did laugh at themselves. I thought this was great of them and the other crew thought it was the funniest thing they had ever been called to. The Patient, when we finally got back to him in the shop had a great laugh as well. He said that he wondered why it had taken so long to get back, he thought we had all buggered off with his leg and forgotten him.

Sunday morning again, Redbourn, to a male believed to be deceased. Knocking on the front door of this house it was opened by a very scantily dressed young lady (I think they used to call them baby doll nightdress) who rushed us up the stairs, to find a middle aged man naked on the bed and obviously dead.

We started asking the usual the questions as to when did she first notice he was unwell? She replied 'Well it's a bit embarrassing, but I suppose it's nothing you haven't heard before. I am up from Tunbridge Wells in Kent and he is from Stratford upon Avon'

She went on 'Well this is the house of a friend of mine, who said we could use it for the weekend. My husband thinks I am in London for the weekend with a girl friend on a shopping trip, his wife thinks he is in Brighton at a conference'

'We haven't stopped having sex since Friday night, and we must have fallen off to sleep sometime after three o clock this morning'

'Ah well' trying to sound knowledgeable and yes this happens every day.

'Don't worry I am sure that the police will deal with this tactfully as they are very good at this sort of thing'

As I am desperately trying to sort this out in my head as my mate looked blankly on or was it the young lady!

'Why the police' she asked

'Well they have to be informed of all sudden deaths and as neither of you live around this area we cannot call his GP out'.

So I sent my colleague down stairs to inform control to call the police as it was a sudden death. The village policeman turned up, but before we went up stairs I told him the story so far, it was now over to him he said.

'Thanks a fucking bunch I have never done anything like this before god knows about tact.

As he walked up the stairs, he was shaking his head from side to side

'Christ knows what I am going to do'

He stopped abruptly as he came face to face with the young lady who still hadn't got dressed! Having told us she would have a good bath after this mess was cleared up! The police called their on call Doctor who came along to pronounce the death so we could leave it in the capably hands of the police. We had been there for nearly two hours, and we made cups of tea for everyone and the policeman had taken all necessary statements he needed. As we started to leave he said 'At least I don't have to tell the wife, that's up to his local police force, and she is the one who would have to keep it all from her husband I think I got out of that rather well.

'Well aren't you a lucky boy then'

His reply to me was 'Bolloxs'

Having just started duty at 1500hrs my old sweat of a crew mate always went straight to the WRVS tea bar at the city hospital. We had just got there when we were told to proceed to an address not far away, to two people, collapsed. We were met by a person outside this house saying he could see a person lying in the hall way and he could smell gas. I broke the door down with my small

168

size 8 shoe, and sure enough the house appeared full of gas. I went straight into the kitchen to find a lady who appeared to have been dead for some time lying on the floor by the cooker. The gas cooker didn't appear to have its taps on!. The man in the hall way was still alive and we conveyed him to hospital straight away, calling for a second ambulance for the deceased.

We met up with the police a couple of days later to ask what had happened at this address. It appeared the police had come to the conclusion that the male patient the husband to the deceased lady had been kept alive by the letter box opened when the newspaper hadn't been pushed through the letter box properly. This is how he managed to survive from the flow of fresh air. To be honest I cannot remember if this was just a gas leak or perhaps a suicide that had gone wrong.

One day the ambulance we were on had broken down with a puncture, and we were waiting for the fitter to come out to us get us mobile again. We could hear control scratching around to get ambulance to a call. Our sister crew became available and they were sent to a woman had fallen down stairs, and there seemed to be some sort of problem with a baby. We heard the crew arrive and then heard the crew ask for the police to come to the scene immediately. We never heard any more over the radio.

When we became mobile again we met up with the crew at the hospital some time later and we asked them about this incident. Having arrived at the scene they said a little girl of four opened the door to them and in a crumpled heap behind the little girl was her mum. She was in a hysterical state as she tried to explain to the crew that she had left her baby in the bath upstairs, it was some time ago she thinks, she was not sure, how long she had been lying at the bottom of the stairs. One of the crew went upstairs to the bathroom to check on the baby whilst the other crew member stayed with mum and set about sorting her out as she had broken her leg. She told him that the phone had rung while she was bathing her baby and she came down stairs to answer it. She told her four old to just to keep an eye on the baby while she got the phone. She remembers coming too with her four year old looking over her. By now the other crew member came to the top of the stairs and signalled to his partner that baby was very dead in the bath. He came down the stairs and told the mother that he was a getting another ambulance for the baby and all is well.

Mum was checked over and they found not only had she a broken leg, an arm and a fractured skull too, she must have been unconscious for some time. Coming to she got her four old to get the phone for her so that she could phone for an ambulance. The second ambulance arrived and they took mum off to hospital whilst they waited for the police for continuity, so they could explain the situation to them. The police concluded, after an investigation it was a very tragic accident. As we have been told so often by the police, don't ever take things for granted if you are unsure of anything always calls us.

As I have said during the ambulance strike, the Army and Police were dealing with all 999 and doctors calls, whilst us officers were attending some calls. I was sent to a call at 00.30hrs, in St.Albans saying two children, were unconscious. I was at home in bed, so I jumped into my uniform and rushed off to the address which was 5 miles away from my home. I was met at the front door by a very concerned father. Taking a quick examination of these two boys I quickly ascertained they were completely drunk! This I believe was quite a shock to their mother who then started looking for alcohol and she soon found two empty whisky bottles. The parents told me they thought one was half empty and the other bottle was a new one.

The 12 year old stared to go into respiratory arrest. The lungs were not taking in air but the heart was still beating. I started cardiopulmonary Resuscitation (CPR). Within 20seconds the 10 year old boy was starting to do the same! Still no help had arrived. I got the mother to ring our control and I got the father to assist me, he took over from me with his eldest son while I started CPR on the younger boy. The mother got through to our control and I told her to ask for a "County" ambulance to attend and if that's a no go please send two police or Army ambulances to this address. A minute went by and I was sweating my ears off trying to ventilate these two boys and I heard an army ambulance drive up, in walked a Royal Navy medic, so I handed him the 12 year old and told him to go straight to casualty at St. Albans and I told the police escort to notify the hospital, that they needed a Doctor standing by for these two boys. Within another minute a police van used as an ambulance turned up and I just jumped in the back of the van and got the driver to rush us off to the hospital. I must admit this job really pushed me to my limits, I was fearful of the outcome a bottle and a half whisky is a lot to consume.

Both boys stomachs were washed out by the usual stomach pump method and survived to fight another day, but some how I don't think their favourite tipple will ever be whisky in the future.

CHAPTER 12:
Assaults and Domestics

As Christmas draws near, so the calls for domestic incidents increase, from November through to the end of January usually? There can be an increase in violence and suicide attempts. The usual problems, of not enough money, whose turn it is to have the mother in law, who do we go to for Christmas etc. The expectation of every one puts undue stress on some families. Even without Christmas, holidays as a whole can be too much for some couples, and even a weekend can even be too long as well.

Sunday evenings, the male partner may be deemed to have not done his DIY or his family chores, either because he has watched too much TV. or has slept in too late on Sunday morning, this can lead to tensions and violence in the home, and of course alcohol is another serious problem that puts a strain and violence into family life

Also assaults in pub fights, or street fights, yes they did happen in my early days, but not on the scale or viciousness as now with knifes and guns.

The day after Boxing Day late evening, the bells go down for the fire service and us to attend a person trapped in a bedroom!, no fire situation though. It was to Colney Heath, a small village a little distance away from the station. So off we went and got to the scene with the police right behind us and the fire service about a minute later. Going into the house we were greeted by two small children at the front door and behind them we could hear a woman screaming. I was not able to understand what was being said or shouted.

I said hello to the children and asked what was going on?

'Mummy and daddy are not happy and they are shouting at each other.'

Well they were right there. A woman was shouting her head off at someone, we where now attracting a large crowd of onlookers, as two police cars, and a fire appliance a fire officer's staff car and an ambulance were all parked in this small road.

A policewoman took charge of the children I went up stairs followed by a police man and a fireman to investigate the screaming. We came upon a woman of about five foot one with a frying pan in one hand knocking seven bells out of a bedroom door! 'Let me in you lazing fucking barstard'

Being a live coward I stopped dead in my tracks and let the police deal with this vicious looking saucepan, the fireman promptly shot off saying 'I'm off to put a ladder up at the window!'

The policeman eventually got the lady to go down stairs with him and that left me to deal with the male in the bedroom.

I called out to the man and saying 'Hello mate I am Gordon from the ambulance service can I be of any help?'

A weak reply came back 'Has she gone yet'

'There's nobody here but me' I said

'Are you sure? She is a fucking evil bitch'

And with a start, I hear him say, 'What's a fireman doing at my window?'

'Your children called us, and told us that he was trapped in the bedroom.'

'I am not trapped' he said 'I ran into here before she fucking killed me.'

'You can come out now as it was all clear.' I told him

He opened the door just enough to see out, I could only see one eye, he was making sure that I was the only person there.

'Are you sure the coast is clear'?

'Honest the police are looking after your wife' I said.

He opened the door and wow! his face was a mess! I gave the thumbs up to the fireman at the window and I made the man go and sit on the bed. My mate passed me the first aid bag and went to get some water to clean this mans face up. His nose was fractured his eyes are swelling up and he had serious lacerations to his forehead, cheeks, lips and I think some of his cheek bones were fractured as well. He said he was not sure what had happened to him. He was also suffering from concussion, we carried him down stairs into the ambulance. We asked the police woman what had happened to him, because, the patient couldn't remember.

Apparently the wife had gone mental, because, as she told us the story

'The lazy fucking barstard has been home since Christmas Eve lunch time, and all he's done is watch the bloody telly, drunk beer, sat on his arse, and hasn't help with the kids, in fact he's done sweet fuck all and he can go and rot in hell. I've had enough of doing everything. I thought I would make him move his fucking arse after I hit him he moved alright! I feel much better now.'

'Looking at his face' I said to her

'Its lucky he got up because if he hadn't, and she hit again, it could be even more serious'

I asked the police what is going to happen to her, they said that it would be up to the husband if he wanted to press charges they would charge her, but said they would wait until they speak to him tomorrow in hospital. On route to the hospital we told him that his wife had hit him with a frying pan because he hadn't done much to help her over the Christmas period. All he did was shake his head and muffled a reply.

'She always complained I got under her feet!'

I felt some sympathy with him, us men never get it right.

Here we go again Sunday morning, called by the police to Verulamium Park St.Albans, two males injured, strange we thought as we moved off to the park. We were met by the police who had one very dishevelled and very wet young male about 17 years old, another male who was holding his arm across his chest and appeared in extreme pain.

We asked, 'What have these two lads been up to then?'

The policeman answered the question.' They decided to attack that man over there with the dogs'

He pointed over to where his colleague was talking to a very smartly dressed man some 20 yards away, he had with him, two miniature poodles. He went on to say

'They thought this man was a homosexual in his mannerism as he walked around the lake with his dogs and thought they would sort him out. That was their big mistake as he was a marshal arts expert. This very wet man was thrown into the lake, and the other young man we think has a broken arm, but that's up to you to confirm'

We checked this mans arm and confirmed to the policeman that he was right in his diagnosis. We waited for another policeman to turn up to accompany these two men in the ambulance as we took them off to casualty. The wet one had to have loads of jabs just in case there was anything nasty in the lakes water, and the other young man had his arm set in plaster and then both of them were then taken off to the police station. The police in those days didn't have the politically correct brigade looking over their shoulders to arrest the man with the dogs as he was the victim, and that's how the police dealt with things.

I heard a call for an ambulance to proceed to a man assaulted at a hairdressers shop in Luton, but was too far away to deal with it. Later on I asked the crew what had happened at the shop. Well they started to laugh; it was really funny they said. We were met at the door of the shop by a police woman who was talking to a sobbing young lady, she pointed to a chair where another lady was attending to a man sitting in the barbers chair.

They took over from the lady who was holding a big wad of cotton wool on his head. They removed this and there was a big laceration to the back of man head bleeding very profusely. They asked him what had happened, he replied that he didn't know. They asked the lady if he had been unconscious and she replied for about a minute. Still no response came from the man about what had happened, so they decided to place him on the stretcher and wait for the police woman to tell them what had occurred there. She came into the ambulance and told the patient and our crew what had happened. It appeared that the young lady was blow drying this mans hair she saw the cape moving up and down where upon she hit the man over the head with the back of the hairdryer.

She pulled away the cape away and yelled at him 'You dirty barstard'

Thinking he was masturbating, but all he was doing was cleaning his glasses!

The poor patient couldn't remember any of this, the laceration was approximately 10cm long and down to the skull, he was kept in hospital for 24hrs. I don't know if the young lady was prosecuted, for an assault or whether he receives free haircuts for the rest of his life from this shop.

Now I am not sure if this call should be in this chapter or in recreational, but here it is. Having been called to a house in Borehamwood, to a woman with a broken arm. As we conveyed her to hospital, I needed to know the history, how she had broken arm. The first story she gave me didn't ring true, that she had fallen over and this did not quite match up with the injury.

Then she said 'Alright I will tell you exactly what has happened to me. I am a prostitute and this particular client gets very excited and very rough, and this time he went too far and broke my arm, please don't tell the police'

I assured her that I wouldn't, it was up to her to inform them if she wanted to. Innocently I said to her

'This could put you off working'.

'Not bloody likely' she replied' the client had given her an extra £150.00 to say sorry for his actions. Some of her other clients she said, would give her extra money for wearing a plaster! I told my colleague what had happened and how much she had received by the way of an apology we said we were in the wrong job as our weekly pay was £17.75 a week!

But as my mate said, 'Perhaps we wouldn't even earn £10.00 a year if we went out on the street'

I guess he was right, ah well back to the day job!

While waiting at the St. Albans Casualty one evening for a patient to be transferred to a London hospital. A male patient walked in to be seen. I told him everyone was busy at the moment, but I would take all his details, and pass it on to the sister when she became free. All us ambulance staff used to help out in "Old days" filling the cards etc, he then becomes very defensive towards me. He appeared a bit effeminate, as I told him it gave the staff some idea how quickly they could see to you. I would take the card straight to them if he told me the problem. He gave me his details, he was from Luton. I asked him what his job was he said he was a plaster technician in a hospital.

So I asked him what the problem was. 'Well I was walking through some woods when two men attacked me and they have stuck plaster of paris up my anus!'

Count to three I said to myself, the most implausible story I have heard in years.

'Ok sir, well first of all would you like us to call the police to report this incident'

He replied 'No thank you'

'Ok sir I will go and let the staff know'

Without thinking I said 'If you would like to take a seat in the waiting room'

He just looked at me as if to say, Up yours. I went off to find the sister who was just finishing off getting our patient ready for London.

'What now?'

She's says to me as I bring the patient card into her. I said that she was going to like this one as I explained what had happened to the man in the waiting room.

'What a load Bull Shit' she says

'Christ if you were going to make a story like that, you wouldn't say your job was a plaster technician would you?'

My colleague who had been helping the sister started to have a fit of the giggles and said ,he stood more chance of being attacked by a group of nuns than man being attacked by two men who just happened to have on them plaster of paris.

Another fit of giggles started when trying to get to the Watford football ground, there had been an incident in St. Albans where a male person had run off from the police after an assault. It appeared that he was in a flat above some shops in the High street and was threatening to use a gun. He kept leaning out of the window of the flat egging the police on. The police were in the progress of waiting for more backup to clear the street plus put in a road block but things were happening too fast. I offered to use my car as well as another one of my officer's cars that had turned up to block off the road.

We did this with our blue lights on as well as the flashing headlights. A motorcyclist tried to weave his way between our two cars, at which point he was unceremoniously grabbed by a police man who asked him

'What do you think these cars are parked across the road for, decoration?'

The motorcyclist just looked at him and said

'Fucked if I know, but they are in my fucking way, and so are you fucking grabbing me like that!'

Luckily for this moron, the police hadn't the time to deal with him and pointed him off in another direction. The police managed to gain access to the premises and take the man with the gun down. Whilst I appreciate I shouldn't start laughing but one, the moron was obviously in a world of his own. Two, how the policeman kept his cool and the presence not arrest him I don't know. But three, why the swearing by the motorcyclist I just could not fathom that out.

CHAPTER 13:
Babies

Now I must admit when I joined the service I never for once thought about delivering babies or for that matter having to bring one into the world. I only managed it with some big help from the mothers to bring fourteen babies in to this world. I can never say I enjoyed it, only after it was completely over and I could be sure Mum and baby were OK. Oh and our training, what training? It was given by "The old boys" who said to me 'Don't worry son its easy, the first thing you do is get the husband to boil loads of water'

'Why' I asked.

The reply stunned me 'So that you get him out of the bloody way!'

The next thing is you hope a midwife is just around the corner to come to your aid and save you all the bother and the worry.

When we did receive some training we were told you never to move a mother who was down to five minutes or less with her contractions. This became more of a problem, as more and more maternity units told the mothers, to wait for their contractions to get down to at least four minutes before they called an ambulance to get them into hospital.

My first delivery came on an Easter Monday, the call was only five minutes away from the station, and on arrival we were met by the husband who rushed us up stairs to a bedroom where some groaning was coming from. On entering the room, the patient was lying on the bed saying its 'Coming'.

I asked if I could look but before I had hardly even got the words out, as I lifted her night dress there was this little foot sticking out of her,

This was going to be my first birth, and a breach birth at that, also I was the senior guy and I had only been in the job two years. I drew a deep breath and calmly said.

'Did you know you are having a breach birth?'

"Yes" was the reply.

I sent my colleague down to get the maternity pack out of the ambulance and the list of midwives on call, we carried in a folder. The list was supplied to us because the hospital would never send any of there midwives out from hospital even if the patient was booked into their unit. He came back with the mat pack which consists of two sanitary towels, large grease type paper to put under the patient and over the bed or floor, and cotton wrap type coat to wrap the baby in. I sent him off to go through the folder supplied to us starting off with nearest midwife to us.

I asked the patient if she had any other children 'Yes three others'

Great I thought at least she knew what was coming more than I did. The husband was asking if there any thing he could do to help. I remember my own old colleague's remarks to get him off your back.

'Yes please could you boil up loads of water?'

He was off like a shot. His wife was having contractions every two minutes and I was asking her not to bear down. 'I am trying not to' she replied

'But if you like you and I can swap places with you'

I just smiled at this not knowing what to say really, but at least she had a bloody good sense of humour I gave her that. In the mean time all was going well, I had managed to get the other foot out and mum and I were working on getting the legs out hoping that any second my mate would turn up with midwife. No such luck.

'We are doing very well' I told mum,

I was out of breath hyper-ventilating, breathing with her through her contractions and pushing. She gave birth to a little boy. By now the dad had returned to the room.

'It's only men that cause problems right from when they are born until, the time they die' She says, as she looked at her husband.

'I am glad to see you are still laughing.' I replied

As I was trying to persuade her to hang on until the midwife got there before she pushes again I could hear myself pleading with her to no avail though I heard the raw of the engine of a Bedford J coming up the road, and she gave out another push, and the baby was now out to its neck. At last I could hear footsteps running up the stairs. Thank Christ for that I say to myself as the midwife walked into the room. She took one look and said, 'Ah well, you've nearly done it all, carry on'

She walked back out of the room saying 'I'll just get my bag'

'No' I shout

'My mate will that bring that up for you' Trying not too sound too panicky.

She came back with a big grin and said she would help do the last little bit!

I am glad she thought it was a little bit. All was delivered safe and sound. Me, I am like a gibbering wreck leaning against the wall for support!

The mother was absolutely brilliant throughout this ordeal. The midwife cleaned the baby and mum up while we waited for the afterbirth and then loaded them all into the ambulance and off we went to the hospital. I was knackered, but the mother she was fine! Any thing after this will be a doddle I thought. This was not for me, whilst it is a great thing to bring a new life into the world, and I know it is a natural thing to happen. We had so little training plus the fact you are dealing with a host of onlookers, the patient who is putting all their faith in you. Also we didn't have the help of gas and air in those days either!

I was to be proved wrong in thinking it will be a doddle from now on, as my other deliveries never seem to go that smoothly either, inside Marks and Spencer's on the shop floor .The staff put cloths stands all around us whilst we worked away to bring this one into world. Every body involved was so happy and as we carried the mum and baby out of the shop there was huge applause! Or like the one we delivered on the top deck of a Double Decker bus. We needed an extra ambulance crew to help us carry the mother down the stairs and the baby was fine. Why do women go out on the day a baby is due. Like the lady who called into the some very nasty public toilets where we were up to our ankles in water. Between the mothers pushes we managed to move the lady to the stairs before we gave up, and had to deliver the baby on the stairs. We moved her into the ambulance to deliver the afterbirth.

My colleague and I had to go home and change our uniforms, and have baths the toilets were that bad.

I had two other deliveries where the babies decided to come out with the cords around their neck. "Boys" as I remember what first the mother had said 'It is only men who cause all the problems.' I was more than agreeing with her by now.

The smallest one, I nearly delivered happened during one of the strikes for better working conditions by ambulance staff. It happened at a motel near Potters Bar. A 17 year old girl who worked as a cleaner at the motel felt unwell, the next thing she knew was this thing being discharged from her! Staff called for an ambulance. Because the ambulance staffs were on strike, I was sent on being only three minutes away from this call and arrived to be met by anxious staff who informed me prior to meeting the patient that she didn't even know she was pregnant!

Entering the room I met a very mystified young girl with the smallest baby I have ever seen. I wrapped the baby up in a hand towel. I called our control and asked if an ambulance with a premature baby incubator would attend this job as the army or a police vehicle would be unable to deal with this safely. The ambulance crews even though they were on strike, would always attend a serious incident without hesitation if asked especially if a child was involved. Whilst waiting for the ambulance to attend I cut the cord and waited for the afterbirth to come. I asked the patient why she didn't know she was pregnant and it appeared she didn't understand how babies were made. So with some intrepidation I explained what happens and with some adding up of days and weeks it appeared this baby was twenty six weeks old or thirteen or fourteen weeks premature.

Thankfully a Hertfordshire ambulance arrived with an incubator and two senior midwives who thankfully took over, and started cleaning the baby and sorting out the afterbirth, they got the mum all cleaned and tided up. I asked the weight of the baby, it weighed in at an astonishing one pound thirteen ounces! They put this little baby into the incubator and along with mum set off to hospital. They went to the QE11 special baby care unit before being transferred to a London hospital later.

I checked up on mum and baby about two weeks later, the baby I was glad to hear that it was holding its own.

Why are things never straight forward when babies come into this world? Three thirty in the morning seems to be the most popular time that babies want to pop out. As we travelled to this address my mate I always asked the same question, why always at this time in the morning. We were met by the mother of the patient who asked us to be as quiet as possible, because they didn't want the girl's father to wake up! We were ushered into this small toilet area, the girl who was just 17 years old had had the baby in the toilet bowl, it was still attached to the cord. The after birth had come as well she told us that she had been there for some time. We got her off the toilet and retrieved the baby and tried to resuscitate. We rushed the mum and baby into the hospital, whilst I worked on the baby. The doctors took over from us and worked hard, but all to no avail. By now her mum and dad had arrived, the father was going ballistic with anger at his daughter saying 'I am going to kill her for being pregnant'

The Doctors came out to speak to him, to try and calm him down, but he wasn't having any of it. The police had to be called and he was removed from the hospital. Some months later I saw in the local paper that at the inquest into the death of this baby. The daughter's father had still not calmed down even then, and he was still saying he was going to kill his daughter.

As this call starts to unfold, this also turns out as the others, not straight forward. As we rang the bell of flat a very pregnant lady answered the door. I was the attendant and I asked the normal questions. As to what hospital she was booked into,

She replied 'Edgware general'

'How often are the contractions' I asked

She looked at me then said 'Your weird asking me these questions'.

I said 'I am sorry if it appeared that way, but we were not supposed to convey you if your contractions are down to five minutes or less'

So I put my next question to her

'Have your waters broken.'

'That's it' she shouted at me

'You're some kind of a pervert, are you getting a kick out of this'

Ops! I thought I'd better step back here, so I let Bruce my partner take over. As we walked her to the ambulance we had to stop as each contraction came. Bruce and I looked at each other and wondered if we were going to make it to the hospital before she had the baby, because if not, I could see serious trouble coming. So he asked her again. 'Are you ok, when is the baby due'.

'Do you get off on this, asking questions?' she shrieked at us.

I drove to the hospital contacting control to inform Edgware Maternity unit we were coming with what we believed to be birth imamate, I put the blue lights on to make progress and I could hear screams coming from the back, knowing that we would have to stop if we had to deliver this baby. You cannot deliver a baby in a moving ambulance. We got into the hospital grounds when Bruce said I would have to stop as it was on its way. She was telling Bruce to keep away from her. I rushed off to get a Midwife, as there was no time to call control to sort it out, this would have caused more stress for the patient if I was their, by now she was not taking a shine to Bruce either.

I found a midwife and rushed back to the ambulance and let the midwife take over with Bruce in attendance. The patient was still not very happy with our presence or the presence of the midwife either. The main thing from our point of view was that the baby was fine and the mother! Well she still carried on in her strange way.

Not surprisingly we never got a thank you or anything else from the patient, Bruce and I had a laugh over it though, his only response which was aimed at me

'Christ Gordon, she summed you up pretty quick didn't she?'

I picked him up later from the A&E dept!

CHAPTER 14:
Planes and Trains

When I joined the service Hertfordshire used to have six aerodromes De Havilland at Hatfield later taken over by the British Aircraft Corporation. It is now a housing and warehouse estate. Panshanger Welwyn Garden City is used by light aircraft. Elstree Aerodrome also only used by light aircraft and helicopters but has about 400 movements a day. De Havilland, Leavesden, Watford, is now a film set for Harry Potter and James Bond movies and business. Handly Page, Radlett are still making up their minds at the moment about what to build on this land but has light industry estate on parts of it. Bovingdon a wartime airfield used up to 1972 and in its later years used as a film set for The Battle of Britain and other war time films. It now houses a prison.

Bedfordshire had five aerodromes, that is now down to four, Luton Airport, Cranfield. Henlow which is owned by the Royal Air Force but only light planes use it now. For outstanding vintage planes The Shuttleworth Collection at Old Warden is well worth a visit and has some really good flying displays. The last airfield that has now closed was Thurleigh, a World War 11 base and after the war used as a research base.

The first plane crash I went to was during an overtime ban, we had to travel from our base in St Albans to Tring. The actual location is called Crong, it sits on a large hill, a distance of some thirty five miles from St.Albans, and we were the nearest ambulance. This location is the highest point in Hertfordshire, we have one of our Ariel masts positioned on this hill, and it has a micro-wave clear line of sight to the Urals in Russia.

It was a horribly night, rain, sleet and fog we were informed that this plane was enroute from Birmingham airport to Leavesden. The Information on how many people were on board. (The proper term used is "Souls" on board) was scant. It had crashed into a wooded area. On our arrival there were four fire appliances plus several fire officers, four police cars and then us!

We walked into the woods in total darkness, apart from small flames coming from the crashed plane. As my colleague and I walked in we sunk up to our ankles in mud, the more we struggled the further we sank into the mud, then we lost our shoes. We spent the rest of the time walking around in our socks.

We found three legs that didn't appear to match up so we thought there must be three people on board. We needed more light, and by pure chance that day Garston Fire Station had taken delivery of a brand new rescue tender in the form of a Range Rover. Whilst we waited for extra lights from that rescue tender, we found a torso still burning. Then all of a sudden all of us stopped what we were doing, because we could hear this noise in the distance getting louder and louder. Then it stopped, then we heard this ladies voice say 'Here you are driver I think I've found the right place for you'

It was the old rescue tender from Stevenage, this was the size of a bus and with the distance it had travelled, it had blown the exhaust off, so apart from it sounding like several tanks it was dragging the exhaust behind it as well! The lady had been stopped by the two firemen, because they were well out of their area and lost. This local elderly lady in her Morris Traveller led the way for them! It was the best thing that could have happened, it helped to humour the moment so we could carry on with this traumatic event. With the extra lighting, we did match up the legs there was only the two persons on board the plane.

We returned to our base having left the deceased at the scene for the police to deal with, minus our shoes, we were caked in mud and soaked through. We had to call in our home address to clean ourselves up.

Leavesden aerodrome an assistance call from an ambulance on scene as a worker had walked into a propeller from an aeroplane that was taxing in to its slot. As you can imagine, it was an horrific sight to witness and several people had collapsed. We were stood down prior to our arrival, as the other ambulance, managed to deal with the incident.

John Cunningham also known as "Cats Eyes as during the WW11 he was an ace night fighter in Mosquito's. He was the Chief test pilot for BAC, he was flying a 146 jet liner, it had developed problem with its landing gear but landed safely. As he alighted from the plane he just smiled and said 'Sorry lads no trade today'

He lived in my town I meet him on several occasions he was a lovely gentleman in every way.

Strangely I was called to his house when his gardener was taken ill, he was running around, not copping very well with the situation, but his housekeeper soon sorted him out and he was dispatched indoors.

Hatfield again this time to a 125 executive jet flown in from France once again it was the undercarriage that had collapsed on landing, causing it to career of the runway and onto grass; fortunately the French crew and passengers were all uninjured.

Landing gear seems to be the biggest problems on planes.

Even though Elstree was a busy little airfield I only attended there three times, it has a very good safety record. This is the airfield where Graham Hill was approaching when he lost his life crashing onto a golf course near the A1 at Arkley between Barnet and Borehamwood. He lived nearby in Shenly. On all those three occasions the planes landed safely, even though one did three circuits to get it right before he landed. The wheel on his starboard wing was facing a 90 degrees angle, but as he landed it straightened up, much too every bodies relief

Luton Airport, a very busy International airport also has a very good safety record.

Mostly the incidents were of a precautionary call. It could just be a warning light coming on inside the cockpit, so the captain has to alert the emergency services, as he couldn't leave any thing to chance. We had a full emergency contingencies plan for this airport and this is still strictly adhered to. Two ambulances and officers, go to the airport, other ambulance are moved into the area where the plane is approaching, in case it falls short. The receiving hospital at Luton & Dunstable would be alerted so they could be ready if needed to bring their emergency plan into operation.

The planes that landed there ranged from light planes carrying one person to the large Boeings and Airbuses carrying up to 230 people.

Among the more the memorable ones I attended, was Tom Cruise in his own executive jet which had developed an engine problem. He was attending Stanley Kubrick funeral. The film Director and producer of Clock Work Orange and Space Odyssey 2001. Stanley Kubrick lived between St.Albans and Harpenden in a very nice Country Estate, and the funeral was being held in Harpenden. As with all calls for problem planes, the airport fire service foam tenders followed the planes to their landing slot. They would check the plane out and then we would be stood down if everything was ok. We never did see any body alight off this plane

As a call comes in to a plane having been hit by birds, I just thought it had taken off it a flock that gather around the grass area, and was coming back into land to be checked out The plane had flown into a flock of geese at 30,000 feet this is an incredibly height for a bird to fly I was also amazed at the damage that this had caused to the nose cone. The Captain was not impressed at these geese damaging his plane, but like me he was amazed at birds flying at that height as he hadn't heard of that before.

But light aircraft are Luton's biggest problem as they can shut down their bread winners the Airlines. Delayed flights can cost Airlines a fortune as well as goodwill. So when a light aircraft had its right undercarriage collapse on the runway. This really upsets the powers in charge certainly wished it hadn't happened. It closed down the airport for hours whilst the Accident Investigation people turned up, and then it can be removed from the runway. We did convey one passenger to hospital with minor injuries from this plane.

So when another light aircraft got into trouble when it's under carriage would not come down on one wing, with all the emergency services now in attendance the plane now only has to land. Once again the airport management are not amused, because they have airliners waiting to land and take off. The pilot was on his own, as he came in to land he changed his mind, and set off to start again.

One liner was allowed to take off while he set off on another circuit. He did this on six occasions, you could see fumes coming out of the airport staffs ears as they had all these planes late on their stands and could not move off until this person landed his bloody plane!. 'He better land the fucking thing now'

Says one operations manager.

I found that funny, what were they going to do to him if he didn't, shot him down? He says he is going to land on to the grass so that the runway was kept clear and it would make a softer landing causing less damage to his plane. This did make the airport staff a bit happier. Otherwise he was going to told to go somewhere else. He came in for his last landing he told them over the radio. He did a good crash landing as skidded on the grass like he said, with no injuries to the pilot. Every one, especially the management was pleased. The airport was now clear to operate again, at last we could all pack our bags and go home!

Luton airport is getting even busier and light aircraft are being persuaded to go else where, even the police helicopter has been moved to the Royal Air Force base at Henlow. The police helicopter had been at Luton Airport since its conception in 1993.

Cranfield aerodrome is used by light aircraft and I got called there on three occasions. Apart from one all the others landed safely. The one that crashed caused the manager of the airfield to ring me the day after the accident. Which like the other light aircraft crashes this involved a wheel collapsing on landing with no injuries. He had rung to say, he had seen on the local television news, the filming of the plane which crashed on his airfield.

'So why ring me' I asked

'Because you were seen with a camera and you had no permission from any one to do this'

'Well if I was seen with a camera' I asked

'Why wasn't I questioned at the time, and for your information I didn't give my video to any one as I was only taking pictures for training purpose'

He went on for some time about this incident and he wanted an apology for it being on TV. I told him that the fire service were there had you asked them. As there was no way I going to give him an apology for something I hadn't done. I suggested he changed his manner when talking to people otherwise he could see himself in court. How to win friends and influence people I thought. I did inform my Director in case he came knocking on his door to ask him, but he didn't.

Apart from the two train fires I have already mentioned I attended two train crashes more or less at the same location but some fifteen years apart. These two accidents happened in Watford just south of Watford junction.

Borehamwood, my colleague and I were about to go off duty, we had just put the kettle on. To make a cup of tea for the oncoming night crew as we were on 1500/2300hrs, shift. And as per usual the phone rings, its control, proceed to Water lane, Watford, believed a Train crash, and it might be a major accident. Now a Major accident in the ambulance service terms is any accident/incident involving twenty five live patients or more. We arrived to find that we were the second ambulance on scene as I was a Leading ambulance man I was then made incident officer, until I hoped that one of our officers turned up.

The first ambulance had six patients onboard with various cuts and fractures but all relatively minor in our terms. They informed me that it was a collision between two trains and that another four ambulances were enroute to the scene. I was talking to the police incident officer and surveying the scene all at the same time, then the other ambulances all rolled up. The scene was a locomotive that had gone down an embankment with a carriage attached to it, several other carriages even though they were upright after the collision with the other train. As I struggled up the embankment to walk along the track and carriages, a policeman who informed me that under one of the carriages was the driver of one of the locomotives but he has no head. Would I just put a blanket over him as it was his first month in the job and hadn't dealt with anything like this.

'Not to worry, he isn't going anywhere' I told him

'I will come back later for him, I'll sort out the living first.'

By this time the senior ambulance officer had arrived, so he took charge of the incident. Between us we made sure all the injured passengers were on the ambulances and removed to Watford General hospital. It was now my responsibility along with my colleague to retrieve the body of the train driver. I got under the train with a pair of stretcher poles and a canvas to lay the poor chap onto the stretcher. The driver was laying face down, and as got to him I thought there's not much blood around if he had been decapitated, as I rolled him over onto the canvas, his head popped out from under is coat! The coat had gone over his head, looking as if he had been decapitated.

The young policeman was over the moon as it was going to be his job to accompany us to the hospital, and the mortuary after he had been certified. We struggled to get the driver from under the train and that was the easy part. Then we had to get him down the embankment to our waiting ambulance, with aid of the firemen and policemen.

The next day having just come on duty at 1500hrs my colleague and I were off to Barnet General Hospital to convey a patient to their home address. Then control called us to return to the station immediately and report to our station officer over the phone. I said to my colleague 'What the fuck have we done now'

As I have said before you only talk to officers when you've done something wrong.

I phoned up the station officer who said 'You must go home straight away and change your uniforms, place them into a bag and then take them to local dry cleaners to be cleaned. You both have been in contact with blue asbestos the train you dealt with last night is full of the stuff.'

I said 'It's too late we had changed our uniforms already, we had got so dirty in oil and dust from the shingle and sleepers retrieving the driver'

He put the phone down on us!

God knows what he was thinking, up to neck in filth, and we would come into work not changing! My wife had already put them in washing machine. After about half an hour he came back to us

'Well I have spoken to people who know about these things and they say you could   be ok so carry on with the job you had been given'

And that was that! We are big enough boys and girls now, we know when to change our clothing and wash our hands!   Or maybe not.

Thankfully not all train incidents are so dramatic, like the. train derailment at Hatfield which was an easy job to deal with. It was a diesel multi carriage, a local train and was only carrying eleven passengers. It was going through a set of points to cross over onto another track and it just came off! We only conveyed two patients to hospital from this incident which was a good result as far as I was concerned

Unfortunately the next accident involving a train was to Leagrave Railway station Luton, a person knocked down. As any one knows you don't normally live after being knocked down by a train. I arrived at the same time as the ambulance and we were directed by railway staff to north of the station about 300yds away. We ensured that it was safe to walk on the line and that no trains were running, because unlike steam trains when I first started in the service, you could hear them some way off. These electric or diesel trains are on you before you know it. By now a policeman had come along to join us, as we walked up the track.

We came across a leg first! Ah it's was going to be a messy job, so I sent one of the ambulance crew back to get a body bag. These are large plastic bag with a zip so you can put bodies in them, they save all the mess in the ambulance. Off he went, and as we walked further along the track we found another leg and the policeman said

'Well that's ok that's the lower bit sorted out'

'Oh no it isn't' I said

'Why not?' The policeman asked.

'Well they are both left legs and unless he had a severe disability that I had never heard of'

'Piss off stop having me on, I don't like these jobs its making me sick already'.

'I am not kidding look at the feet they are both left feet'

'It can't be, the train driver said he only hit one person'

'Well lets walk some more and see what else we can find'

Sure enough we found two torsos further on up the track. We took these two bodies back to the ambulance and then onto the hospital for certification.

I learnt later that week, it was two young men who were taking a short cut back to their house having been shopping for beer, the driver of the train thought he had only hit one person and was not aware that there were two people when he was questioned latter by the police

This unfortunate incident involved workmen on the track, as I had a phone call from control at about 0200hrs whilst I was tucked up in bed and not on call! It was to assist the on call duty ambulance officer, to rail workers hit by a train. He needed Paraguard stretchers or Neil Robinson stretchers. These stretchers are used to place patients into so they can be rescued from situations that need the patient to be strapped in, and then they can be lowered or carried up or out of a building, roof, ditch or in this case an embankment, in any situation where a normal handling situation would not be sufficient to keep the patient immobile.

The location was near Chorleywood Bottom on the Metropolitan line. Now I must admit this is not an area I know very well, but luckily the on call officer lived a couple of miles from this location so he was on the scene pretty quickly. He had found the scene in total darkness and found that he had four railway workers dead at the side of the track. Whilst I was enroute I was kept informed by our control and why he needed these stretchers it was because the location was high up an embankment. It was going to be the only way down, onto the road were the ambulances were parked up. I had to call in to two ambulance stations enroute to him to pick up the four stretchers that he needed.

By the time I had reached the scene, details of how this tragic accident had happened had been worked out. It appeared that a railway wagon used further up the track by other workmen had broken free and started to roll away down the track. It was a decline from where it had broken free, nearly two miles away, and so as it gathered up speed, it would have been very quiet as it ploughed into these unsuspecting workmen. They would not have heard or felt its approach due the work they were carrying out on the track.

With assistance of the Fire and Police we got all four men down off the track and down this embankment into the ambulances.

Déjà vu as I was called to train crash at Watford near to the previous location I attended. I was on my way home and it was around 1725hrs when I got a phone call from the Staff officer telling me to attend a train in a ladies back garden! The address was Ebury Road Watford.

Whist enroute to the scene I called upon more officers to attend the incident,

This was requested by the Staff officer for me to do as control were busy mobilising ambulance to the scene. As I was nearly home, I had just called my wife to say I would be home in five minutes! So she could start getting my dinner ready, not that I demanded it she liked to have it ready for me AH! I here you say.(I got my dinner at around ten thirty that night.)

As I arrived the London Helicopter (HEMS) was landing. The emergency services on the a whole had a lucky break as on one side of the embankment of this railway track was a big field so all the emergency vehicles had plenty of space to park up. On the other side of the embankment was a row of terrace houses where the call had been made from.

Having climbed up to the top of the embankment I was met by two ambulance crews who had been there for about five minutes before me. They started to brief me on what they had found so far. As they were giving me a sitrep as to what they had found, I was surveying the scene. In front of me was an overturned train carriage and behind it was a carriage that had concertinaed and looked like an archway which you could walk under. The fire service had put ladders up onto the overturned carriage so I ordered one crew to get inside and check it out for any injured passengers. I then got a phone call from my control asking if I was going to declare this a major incident.

It appeared that there were well over twenty five passengers milling about with various cuts, abrasions and other injuries, so that was an easy decision to make. There was some edginess in the controller's voice as to why I had given him a sitrep early, but I hadn't been there long enough to inform him of what was what. I had to climb up the embankment and meet up with the crews and survey the scene. I could understand why he was edgy and pressing me for information because it was his responsibility to get the major incident plans into operation. He had to inform the local hospitals to get more resources in, inform the Chief Officer, and inform neighbouring ambulance services in case they were needed for back up. L.AS didn't need asking twice, and if necessary call extra crews in from home. Last of all, we would need a dedicated team of control staff allocated to deal with this incident only. Every thing that is done and said over the radio or phone has to be recorded on a separate log for any court of enquiry that may arise in the future.

Once the crews got to work and more officers turned up to assist me I went back down to ground level and thankfully met up with a police sergeant, who I have known for years, which was the best thing that could have happened to me in this situation. I had found a group of injured passengers on the road side on the opposite to be were everybody had parked up. With the help of this sergeant he gave me spare policemen to drive the Patient Transport ambulances, with the walking wounded passengers to hospital, whilst the two ambulance people on each PTS vehicle tended to the patients injuries. For me, it dealt with a large number of walking wounded straight away. It also helped the sergeant and his team in doing some thing useful, as for the first few hours, a policeman's job can be quite thankless, standing around whilst us, and fire service get stuck into the rescue.

It was great team work and could only be achieved by us knowing each other on first name terms. As per normal on these occasions, I was not getting all the radio messages of what was going on elsewhere by some of my officers. I was informed that there was a large group of injured passengers at Tescos super store in the opposite direction to where we were all situated. These passengers had been sent in that direction by rail staff. At the time I didn't know about this instruction given by the rail staff, I would have been over ruled if had objected anyway. It was deemed it would have been too traumatic for the passengers to have walked past all the damaged carriages to the emergency service rendezvous point! Tescos staff did a magnificent job in taking care of all these people. My mobile rang and I was taken by surprise when I found out it was Sky news asking if they could talk to me in about 5 minutes. How they got my phone number I have no idea.

At last when the scene was clear of all passengers and all patients, the final count of all the injured we had dealt with and conveyed to hospital was seventy patients. One female was fatally injured, 3 patients seriously injured, and two of these were taken by helicopters to the London hospital. At the quick debrief after the incident for me and my staff, we felt it had gone reasonably well. There were some minor mistakes mostly down to me but none that led to any patient not being treated properly, which I considered to be our number one purpose. All the services, Police, Fire, Helicopter medical crews, London ambulance service, and Watford General hospital, all worked well together. I never did find out if the original caller did have this train in her back garden!

When the joint services debrief took place there were some good constructive criticisms of some of the things that happened on that day, by all the services it was overall considered to be a success. One of the things that I was grateful for as it was mentioned in the final report, was the cooperation by the police sergeant in making his drivers available for me to drive the ambulance to hospital. As one police chief Superintendent said to me after the debriefing,

'You have re-written the major incident plan again Enstone!'

How to win friends, etc.

CHAPTER 15:
Road Traffic Accidents

Obliviously I have been to countless Road Traffic Accidents and there are too numerous to go through and to be quite honest I have forgotten more than I am going to relate in the this book, but there are a few that I will never forget mostly for the wrong reasons, because they mostly turned out to be fatal.

Thankfully over the years deaths from road traffic accidents have been reducing and there are many reasons for this. There used to be a tally on the TV news, over Bank holidays of how many people had been killed. It was becoming a National sport!

When the M1 was first built there was no central barrier and no speed limit, and as the traffic built up there was a significant increase of cross over accidents from one carriageway to the other resulting in head on accidents. These head on accidents were some times at speeds of well in excess of over 200mph! So the Armco metal crash barriers came to the rescue, and were soon adopted by all motorways and other main roads. But that did not stop the bigger lorries that started to be introduced onto the roads. Now slowly concrete central barriers are being built on all our motorways to stop lorries ploughing through the Armco barriers like butter.

The fire service, or as they like to be called now, Fire and Rescue services have new techniques as they have had to deal with more entrapments also new and specialised Equipment have been brought, has seen them release people far more quickly from cars and lorries than ever before.

When I first started off, I dealt with two lorries in collision on the A6 at London Colney. I was on an overtime shift that started at 0700/1500 hr and carried on until 2300hrs, but at 2230 this call came in to deal with two Lorries. On arrival it was evident that we needed the fire service to release one of the drivers. They promptly turned up and set about the rescue. After an hour of getting nowhere they asked the police to call up one of the breakdown specialists to come to the scene and bring any equipment they might have for repairing cars with them, because what they had was inadequate.

I was with the driver all the time, and his condition was getting worse and he kept asking me if he was going to die. I tried to reassure him he was going to be ok. The police couldn't get their doctor on call to come and help this poor man, and it was unheard of for a hospital doctor or GP's would turn to help. So we struggled on as best as we could. After fours hours the driver was released, but not before the he had died in my arms after giving up the struggle to live after three. As I look back on that incident, I know with certainly the driver would have been out within an hour, and now we have paramedics or a Doctors to call on

The use of seat belts and more importantly children's car seats, are a good safety precaution although some parents don't seem to care about this small investment. It makes me so angry when I see young children jumping around in a car or sitting on parents laps not strapped in, or the person holding the baby might be strapped in but the baby is not. If only these people knew or even cared what disfigurement or death could happen to these children.

Prior to seat belts the injuries to people's faces were terrible and many needed plastic surgery. Children shot from the back seats into the dash board which left imprints on their heads, and faces from the car radio knobs, also jaws severely damaged from the gear leaver, that what makes me so angry.

I was in my marked up Staff car one day, when I followed a woman home, after I had dealt with a serious injury to a child, who like her child that I was observing as I drove behind her, was not belted up or in car seat. I wanted to tell her what I had been to, so I asked her why she was she letting her child jump around inside the car while she was driving along, not only that it was dangerous for the child but could distract her from driving properly and cause her to have an accident. I know I shouldn't have done it but I was so bloody annoyed to say the least. At least she didn't tell me to Foxtrot Oscar (Fuck off) but by the look in her face and I think she wanted to.

Crash helmets for motorcyclist were made compulsory in the seventies and this was well over due. Before this motorcyclist, who by choice did not wear helmets, could have a relatively minor accident, would often receive facial injuries, and fractured skulls. This act alone saved many a young person's life.

Cars are better designed now, with their crumple zones taking the impact from a collision. Airbags when they work are brilliant, I have been to a few incidents where the airbag had not been deployed. But when they have worked they have saved disfigurement to people.

The reduction of the speed limit was due to the wars in the Middle East and the petrol crisis, I am not so sure that these speed limits are realistic with the modern cars on the road now. I can hear the green lobby and safety groups going ape to what I have just said.

When I first joined the ambulance service there were over 6000 people being killed each year on the roads, now there are just over 3000. Car ownership has gone up and we travel more miles per year now than we ever did. We have lowest death rate in Europe per car miles. Of cause one death is too many, but more women die of breast cancer per year.

When the drink and drive laws, were first introduced in 1967 I was on a night shift. It was really strange, because that weekend there were hardly any cars on the road, and not one call came into our control room to a RTA anywhere in west of Hertfordshire. When they did start to trickle in at night we found that people had ran off prior to our or the police arrival. It was the older generation who thought they knew best and they wouldn't stop drinking, now it's the younger generation that are taking no notice of this law.

Also medical intervention by better trained ambulance staff, first on the scene handing over to better trained doctors and nurses is saving more lives. This has had a knock on effect in a different way, on fewer donors for transplants, and plastic surgeons not doing so much rebuilding work.

Last of all I would like to point out that the ambulance service Does Not Charge for taking you into hospital if you have been involved an RTA. Even if you go by taxi, bus, bike, pram, walk or by the police car or by helicopter you will still be charged by the hospital. This was first introduced when the NHS was first started in 1948 to recoup some of the cost of treating patients, because the health service was only primarily set up for people who were taken ill. When I left the service the standard charged by hospitals was £21.00 per person, but they could charge up to £5,000.00 for initial medical care, and that is why you pay car insurance to pay for this cover.

I don't think a week went by without dealing with an RTA on one of the three motorways, our service covered. The M1 from junction 13 in Bedfordshire to the Gateway service station on the M1 Southbound, just on the outskirts of London. Northbound from junction 5 in Hertfordshire to junction 14.in Buckhamingshire a total distance of approximately 78 miles. The busiest part of the M1 having 160,000 vehicle movements per 24hours is from junction 10 Luton to the M25 junction 6. The M25 from junction 17 through to 26 clockwise and 25 to 16 anti clockwise, a distance of approximately 54 miles, and the whole of the A1M from South Mimms to north of Baldock all through Hertfordshire, and 6 miles of the M10 at St Albans.

Every body says to me. 'Oh you must have been to nasty accidents, especially on the Motorways'. Yes they do seem to more spectacular, but more fatalities happen on other roads.

The biggest and most spectacular RTA, I have been involved in and the longest day was on M1 the date was September 9th 1969. Forever printed in mind. Over 370 vehicles were involved in collisions, in freezing dense fog from junction 10 to junction 7 on the southbound carriageway, with only minor bumps on the north bound carriageway spread over a distance of over 9 miles.

Each ambulance was given a specific accident to attend to as there were so many accidents, we were told if we came across an accident whilst on route to ours we had to report them back to our control and another ambulance would be dispatched to it. As you can imagine apart from the poor visibility, the icy roads enroute from St.Albans going along the A5 to the M1 were extremely treacherous, I had real trouble on travelling along the icy roads and we could only muster a top speed to our allotted accident in safety, at some points of only 25mph, and people were still passing us! As they did so we came across them crashed into the stationary traffic!

They must have thought as they overtook us with our blue light on, why are they going so slowly it can't be that serious where they are going. We drove in and out of the traffic because even the hard shoulder was taken up with vehicles, (this does not happen nowadays as drivers understand what the hard shoulder is for) we lost count of the number of collisions we came across but quite a few thankfully were damage only.

We could only call our control and give the number of vehicles involved and the rough location. Our accident involved a car transporter loaded with brand new Jaguars cars, a Bentley, an Aston Martin and several other cars. The Aston Martin driver jumped on us as soon as we stopped and started shouting at us

'Why has it taken you so long to get here?, and if its going to take you as long to get to the hospital I will take my son my self'

I just looked at this Pratt and replied as I quickly looked around at the scene of this accident.

'You will have a job as you have got no front wheel on your car. Now can I get on with looking after your son please Sir?'

He just went on and on but I just ignored him from then on. Unfortunately, the police were not on the scene, as like us, they were struggling with the resources to attend all the accidents that had happened and still happening in the freezing fog.

We loaded this young lad on to our ambulance along with several other injured people from the accident, but the Aston Martin driver stayed at the scene. Most of the patients that day ended up at Hemel Hempstead General Hospital. We unloaded as quickly as possible and went back again to the motorway. All in all we did three trips that day, which doesn't sound a lot, but the time involved in getting to each accident, putting up with abuse from drivers, had taken us nearly two and half hours for each accident.

Our last call that day we attended, involved a Heavy goods lorry, (HGV) loaded with coal. The driver had been trapped for some time. We arrived just as the fire brigade were about to release him from the cab of his wrecked lorry.

That was how bad that day was for us and everybody else, the police were just overwhelmed with the scale of it all. We had our first call at 0900hrs as we came on duty and finished worn out with nothing to eat all day, at the hospital at 1600hrs.

That was my biggest RTA involving the number of vehicles. My next big one was many years later but that was one only 171 vehicles!

Just south of junction 5 on the M1, a car had collided at speed into the rear of a HGV that had stopped to protect an earlier accident that had happened. The driver had run down the carriageway to warn approaching drivers to slow down and to move into another lane. As he was doing this a car with four people in it, waved at him (he and the police could only presume they thought he was just waving at people as they drove past) the car went straight into, and under the rear of this driver's lorry. All four occupants were killed outright, the front seat female passenger had her skull punctured so hard that it pushed her brain out in one complete unit onto the rear parcel shelve. The crew who I knew very well, who were going to be the ones that conveyed this lady to hospital, asked me to pick the brain up for them and place it in a bag!

A month before, I attended another accident on the M25. I was travelling home when I noticed a lorry in front of me that had its rear off side wheels going in and out of the rear axle, its one of those things that you take a double take at, because you ask your self am I seeing things? But no I was right, it was going in and out as I thought. I started to slow down and pull back from the lorry, because if the whole axle with the wheels came off it could cause a serious accident. I knew there was a roundabout 300yds away, so my intentions were to wait for him to get to the roundabout then I would put my blue lights and siren on and pull him up and inform the driver of the situation with his lorry. I was too late, the wheels and axle came out and bounced over a car transporter travelling in the opposite direction bouncing into a field. The lorry slid to a halt, the driver of the car transporter was either unaware of what had happened or didn't want to be involved as he carried on. In my opinion it was a lucky escape for everybody involved.

But no such luck to the incident I attended on the M25 a month latter. I was called to persons trapped between junction 21A and 22, I was at junction 19 going in that direction when I noticed a police car with all his lights on, so I just tucked in behind him and arrived quickly. It was a one vehicle accident, the car was in lane three with the engine compartment and roof squashed as though a heavy weight had been dropped on it. With difficulty I managed to get inside the car, only to find a young female dead. The fire service and an ambulance arrived, they all got to work to retrieve this unfortunate young lady from the wrecked car. Talking to the police it appeared from witnesses, that a car was overtaking a lorry when a wheel sheared off the lorry and bounced onto the young ladies car. The lorry may have been unaware of what had happened and never stopped. The police launched a thorough investigation into the accident to try and trace the lorry and its driver. But although they never traced either one of them, they discovered the lorry would have been a Scania lorry and it would have been registered in Europe.

On junction 5 M1, at Berry Grove a beer tanker turned over onto its side as it left the slip road. As it did so, the drivers cab fell onto the Armco barrier, decapitating the driver. The fire service managed to free the rest of the body of the lorry driver. As the policeman and ambulance crew were fairly new I ended up in the back of the ambulance whilst the attendant followed us into hospital in my car! I also remember the young female doctor at Watford general was taking aback at what she had to certify.

On junction 6, the M25 interchange with M1, on one Saturday afternoon, a minibus overturned on the long curve from the M1 onto M25 going towards Heathrow. It contained six Asian men. On my arrival there were already two ambulances on scene and another three enroute. There were some heated exchanges going on with the less injured men as to the way their friends were being dealt with by female ambulance crews. The police and I were trying to fathom out the problem. The problem was, they didn't want females touching their friends. But as the police and I told them it was unfortunate that they felt that way, but there was nothing going to be changed in the way they were going to be transported to hospital. They could not stay on the motorway and pick and chose who took them to hospital. Very reluctantly they all got into the ambulances and went off to hospital. One of the men had been killed as the mini bus overturned by his knife he was carrying presumably a ceremonially knife. It had gone straight into his groin and pieced his artery and he bled to death in minutes. I was worried about any problems that might arise at the hospital, so I and a policeman went off to the receiving hospital to insure that all was well with my crews. There were no further problems involving our crews, but now a new problem had arisen which was going to be the hospitals, that the A&E doctor was a female.

There has been a problem with some male Asians, who for some reason cannot accept females treating them. And it goes the other way as females don't want males looking after them. I remember having to go to a seminar with my Director in trying to persuade the Asian community to be employed as ambulance staff. We were told to go to the mosques, and speak to the Immams to recruit staff that way. Before I even took this route I was told by several Asian men not to even bother, as your job back home is looked upon as the lowest of the low, no matter how I explained the job, it would not be accepted by them. I am sure this cannot be for the whole of the UK.

I have already mentioned the weather can play havoc on the motorways, In 1990 there was a very stormy day with gusts of winds up to 80mph, and on the M1 between junction 10 to 8 north and southbound it was causing havoc to the traffic. One of my officers was getting out of his car to deal with an overturned lorry when the door of his car was just taken out his hand by the wind and blown back onto the wing causing severe damage to his arm and the car.(or should I put that the other way it makes me look caring!) It had pulled all the muscles in his arm and he was off work for a month.

As I was enroute to accidents I was amazed at the strength of the wind, and as I followed a lorry on the A5 towards the M1 the driver was having serious difficulty in holding on to the steering wheel, as the lorry was being blown sideways he was trying to park up in a layby. That afternoon we dealt with 16 Lorries that had been blown over by the severe winds. It was also very bad for our ambulances causing them problems as they were being buffeted by these strong winds. Not only that, but they were having difficulties in getting to the scene as well. There were a number of trees that had been blown down across the roads. One ambulance started off from St. Albans ambulance station and was turned back onto a different route; it took three attempts before he made it to the M1.Then he had to wait on the way to hospital whilst a tree was cut up in front of him to enable him to get the patient to hospital. One ambulance was escorted by a game keeper over his estate, because he could not make progress along the main A5 because of the number of trees that had been blown down their as well. They said it was a bit bumpy in places but at least they got their patient to hospital although it was nine miles further. Some people think we have a magic wand and we can get to all incidents even in bad weather, they don't think it affects us as well.

On that day we had to deal with two accidents where two large trees had been blown down on top of two passing cars killing the occupants outright.

For some unknown reason some people say that they do not wear a seat belt in case the car catches fire after an accident and won't be able to get out. I only ever went to two car fires. I can only recall six others. In my experience very few cars do catch fire following an accident. Normally if the car catches fire following an impact, the car is so seriously damaged, that the occupants would be seriously injured and unable to undo the seat belt. On the M1 between junction 13 and 12, a car had been in collision with a bridge, after colliding with another car. It had bust into flames almost immediately, and killed the male and female passengers. The post-mortem report concluded the impact of the bridge killed them prior to the car catching fire.

The other fire situation was not on the motorway, but just outside my home town of Harpenden, on A1081 going towards Luton. A car had failed to stop at a road junction and collided with a car into the side of the car, by the petrol filling pipe. It hit at such a force spinning it across the road and catching fire causing the female to be burnt to her death. The policeman would not believe me, when I told him that the body was a woman. Unfortunately it was, and what made it worse was when they found out who the driver worked at St. Albans police station.

The other rare thing that people always imagine happens a great deal, is amputations following entrapments, in cars and lorries following a collision or accidents. This as I say is very rare and this has only happened once in my career.

On the M1 junction 9 to 8 Redbourn to Hemel Hempstead, four HGV had collided with each other. The fire service was having a torrid time in rescuing one driver. As time was getting on they said that they thought this poor guy would have to have his leg amputated to be able to get him out. Now these firemen are very qualified in dealing with entrapments and for them to say they are having problems then you have got to believe them. Because of this we had a medical team sent from the Luton & Dunstable hospital. The doctor, the fire officer and I conferred and the doctor said he we would give it up to two hours before he made a further decision as the driver was holding up well. But by the time two hours was up it was more than apparent not much progress had taken place, in rescuing him from the cab of his lorry. The doctor reluctantly said that the leg was going to have to come off. He got into the lorry and told the driver about the situation he was in, and that the only way he was going to get out of this cab was by having his leg removed. He explained that he was going to cut it from just below the knee which was just exposed enough for the doctor, and he hope by doing this his prognosis for keeping his thigh bone would make him mobile quicker for getting out of hospital and back to a near normal life as possible. The operation was over and done with in less than 5 minutes, brilliantly done by the doctor. Then it was all hands to get the driver out of the cab with as much care as possible. The driver was then rushed into Hemel Hempstead Hospital. Whilst I had only been in the service seventeen years then, that is still the only time I have been involved in any kind of amputation to free a person from any kind of entrapment. As I have said the skill of the fire service with all their equipment now is second to none. We only took one other lorry driver to hospital from this accident with serious injuries.

Once again the magic Sunday, lunchtime just as my wife was about to serve lunch for the family, the phone rang and it was the control manger informing me of an RTA on the M25 between junction 22 to 23, London Colney, towards South Mimms. It appeared to be a multiple RTA. They were sending two ambulances and there were reports of persons trapped. Off I went arriving to find one lorry on its side lying across the whole width of the carriageway and three cars that had driven straight into the roof of the Trailer unit. Standing next to the lorry were a crew in red suites who I recognized straight away as the LAS Helicopter (HEMS) I notified them who I was, and said I was surprised to see them here as my control were unaware that they were called. You might think by what I have said, that I was annoyed to see them there, that's not strictly true, what annoyed me, was people turning up at incidents with out telling the appropriate authority what's going on, especially the police who have a special system for letting helicopters land on motorways. The system the police use is to stop traffic from passing the scene as the helicopter lands, because the traffic on the opposite carriageways start looking at what's going on instead of the traffic in front of them and that's causes other accidents. If at all possible the traffic is stopped at the proceeding junction until the scene is clear of the helicopter completely. So as I carried on talking to the HEMS crew, they told me I only had one person with an ankle injury. We walked around the lorry towards their helicopter for them to go back home and I noticed a Jaguar salon car with roof completely flattened. It was level with the bonnet and boot. I looked into the car and saw a male driver and female passenger dead. By this time the HEMS crew were about to take off, at no time had they mentioned to me about these two people.

I met up with my crews and a police inspector, we talked through the incident and how many patients were to be conveyed to hospital. The inspector said that the couple in the Jaguar looked like they were either going or just coming back, from a wedding as there was a wedding dress and wedding presents in the boot. After the scene was cleared of all patients, the police had now worked out what happened. The lorry was proceeding from junction 23 towards 22 and had crashed through the central crash barrier, and as it did so it rolled onto its side the Jaguar had gone underneath it crushing the roof onto the two occupants and killing them instantly before coming out the other side. The other cars had crashed into the unit trailer, thankfully it was empty so their injuries were slight.

I find out several days later from the police inspector that the deceased couple were husband and wife, the man being a Vet and the Female a veterinary nurse. They had only just got married on the Friday in the West Country and they were on their way back to their home in Essex.

One of the main accident black spots on the M1 was near to junction 9 on the southbound carriageway just near to Watery Lane Bridge I have lost count of the number of multiple accidents, thankfully mostly damage only. This was the location that I attended that resulted in my wife not getting her medication.

And once again it's a bloody Sunday (Any suggestion on this phenomenon a post card to) It all started out with my wife having been continuously sick for about three days. Having checked with our GP to see what we could do for her, he suggested some medication I could get from the chemist. I booked out with control at about 0945hrs, as I was on call. I had only gone about 200yards from home when, control called me, reports are coming in of an RTA on the A1081 between Harpenden and Luton involving a tanker and several cars. So off I go, and as I got out of the town centre I was surprised to come across a bank of thick fog! This nearly brought me to a standstill as it was so thick. I was first on the scene of the accident. I found it involved one lorry and two cars. I located three patients not seriously injured, and one ambulance would be sufficient to deal with these patients in taken them to hospital.

Having spent over 40 minutes on the scene I moved off and as I could not go past the accident to go back home I decided I to go via the M1.I got only three hundred yards when I came across another accident involving two cars. It was still very foggy and it was difficult to warn other drivers of my presence, even though I had all my light on. Drivers are bearing on you and missing you by inches, because they don't bloody think. I ascertain that only one child was injured so I wait for the ambulance to arrive.

Once again, warning control that they must inform the attending crew to take great care when attending the scene because of the foggy conditions. Not that they needed to be told, it's to warn them really of other road users not thinking. That incident duly dealt with, I moved off again trying to think of a chemist to call into. I proceeded onto the motorway getting on at junction 10. The fog had lifted and it was a bright sunny day! Well until I got to Watery Lane Bridge near to junction 9, one second I was in bright sunshine the next in thick fog, but could see the fog bank so it shouldn't cause too much of a problem. As I came out the other side of the fog I was just about to exit the motorway at junction 9 when I noticed an accident in lane three.

I went over to the scene to see what the problem was; once again calling control to send the police and an ambulance to my location. The quip came back.

'Cant you just go home and leave us alone?'

Whilst I was waiting for the cavalry to arrive, so I could proceed on my merry way to get my wife's medication, a motor cyclist stops next to me and says

'Hi mate you had better get your arse, back up there, there is a fucking almighty big accident'

I looked around me and realised that there were no vehicles on my carriageway. So once again I called up control that it had all gone quiet at my location, but I have been informed that there could be a multiple accident prior to my location. I was setting off on foot to investigate. The fog was moving. One second you could see the next you could not see more than 50 feet. I got to the front of the accident to be confronted with all three lanes completely blocked by damaged cars. I went from car to car still walking north wards I informed control that this was a major incident and to send as many ambulances as they could initially, asking for assistance from another officer at least. I told all the patients that I came across, I would come back to them as soon as possible. I was trying to establish what injuries there were, and how many ambulances were needed. As I was doing this, the sun started to come out and this lifted the fog, I could then see the whole scene. Cars up the embankment, cars over turned, cars slammed sideways into each other, and nose to boot in others.

Coming towards me was one police car, the observer was walking along side the car surveying the scene as he went. We meet up with each other, he said

'Christ what's happened here?'

I said 'I think there's about twenty five plus injured, three seriously, but not likely to prove and I have come across about seventy cars'.

'Well' replied the policeman

'So far I think its about 7 patients and thirty cars up there',

As he points further north of my location. I was told by control that six ambulances were enroute and one further officer. My director, Bob was going into the control room to give assistance to the control staff. The traffic policemen said

'What a bloody awful Sunday this was, why do these things happen when there is the least cover'

At least I knew that everyone who could spared were on their way. The problem Bedfordshire police had, was diverting the traffic off the motorway so we could concentrate on dealing with our accident. But the A1081 was blocked because of the two accidents that had been dealt with only minutes before. I started dealing with the more seriously injured patients, noting the location that I wanted the ambulances to come to first which was not easy. The ambulance crews who were trying to get to my location were having to weave in and out of all the damaged cars, noting what cars they had been instructed to attend to first, by what I had told control. Soon I had the assistance of another officer and we got all the patients sorted, and ready as ambulances arrived to take them off to hospital.

When the scene was clear of all patients, I met up with the senior police officer who I knew very well, and he said to me 'How the hell did you get here so quick ? And where did you get all those ambulances from?'

I said 'You really don't want to know but I will tell you'

I explained everything since I left home.

'I might have fucking known you had something do with all this!'

Laughing as he said it. He said. 'Look go home, check on your wife and we will meet up at the motorway police base and have a quick debrief'

I got home at about1330hrs to find my wife still tucked up in bed waiting for her medication which I hadn't had time to sort out. I made her a hot drink then went to see the police to take stock of what when and how etc. the number of cars involved was 150, the number that had to be towed away was 61, and we conveyed thirty five patients to hospital of which only two were serious.

As always, everyone had worked closely together and had done a magnificent job.

It's the team work one came to expect from each other. The ambulance crews who managed to turn around quickly at the hospital to come back to the motorway and the control staff in coordinating the ambulances to the accidents. We all patted ourselves on the back and went home.

As for my wife, well she's still talking to me! But never did get her medication.

Watery Lane Bridge on the M1 once again, but this time it only involved thirty cars. But we still conveyed nineteen patients to hospital. What people have got to realise is that you can only convey one stretcher patient at a time and at a squeeze three walking patients but only if they are relatively minor injuries. So it's the logistics of getting the ambulances to the accidents, and carrying on dealing with other emergency calls. As more and more hospitals close, the distance ambulances have to travel to hospital, from the motorways get longer, and are as I have said earlier a control manager's nightmare.

For a change it became the M25's turn to have a multiple accident between junction 25 and 24. This involved Seventy two vehicles including many HGV's. For some unknown reason, my Director, Bob was first on the scene! This is partly LAS ground as the border goes in and out all across this section, so we had their assistance as well as our own ambulances. We had four lorry drivers trapped in their cabs and ten car drivers with minor injuries. By the time all the scene was cleared Bob and I drove back towards Junction 24 and 23 checking on people who had been stopped by the police on the opposite carriageway going past the scene. It was a very hot day, as   we checking on people's welfare, in case of distress from the heat or any ladies having a baby! This may seem a strange thing to say but I have known a colleague of mine who came across one lady giving birth on her own in a traffic jam on the M2 in Kent.

One Good Friday night at 2300hrs I had just booked on duty, I was called to an RTA in my home village at the time of Redbourn, in the High Street. I was on with a new crew mate but he was not new to the service. As we arrived the scene looked like a war zone there were cars all over the place. I jumped out of the cab and my crew colleague went to one car and I went off to the other. I was amazed at the damage to these two cars, the impact must have been tremendous. As I looked into one car I found two people deceased. One of them was a female who was tucked up under the dash board. Something I had never ever seen before, and to be quite honest, I was going to leave her there, because at first I thought it was just a coat dumped on the floor. There were also two other very seriously injured people in the car. I ran back to my ambulance to report on the radio that I needed an extra 3 ambulances to the scene. My colleague was dealing with one other person who was seriously injured.

For me it was very strange as I knew several of the people involved, and quite few of the on lookers as well. But my colleague and I got on with job in hand and as the extra ambulance arrived we got the patients loaded and off to the hospital. The police looked after the deceased until the arrival of an ambulance from Dunstable, Bedfordshire which in those early days to have an ambulance come from a neighbouring service was unheard of.

The whole village was stunned by this accident, it ended up with four people being killed and it left several children orphaned. There was a great coming together of the village that raised funds for the children who had lost their parents in the accident.

Occasional there are some funny stories from the accidents we attend which helps make up for the serious ones ones.

Berkhamptead ambulances were called to a car gone into a shop window. Only two patients were conveyed to the hospital and these were the two occupants of the car. But the story behind this RTA was the funny part.

The two female's, the driver and passenger had been staying at Champneys Health Farm, this is a world famous retreat used by people to detoxify, lose weight, get fit and be thoroughly pampered etc. They had decided to take a day out and as they drove through Berkhampstead they saw this wonderful cake shop. They said they had been taken by the display of all those delicious looking cakes which they had missed during their stay at the Health farm. The driver just drove straight into the shop window.

When they handed the patients over to the hospital one of the women said to our crew

'What's so frustrating, that we still never got one of those delicious cakes!'

I don't think the following couple saw this incident as funny as we did though. RTA on the A5 Radlett, a car on top of another car, persons reported (trapped) As we rushed off at full throttle hoping to get to the scene before the Fire Brigade, but knowing that there was a retained fire station just down the road and it was not going to be possible. We arrived on the scene to be met by the officer in charge of the fire appliance who had a big smile on his face. He said that no one was trapped and the injured people a male and a female were only slightly injured, but they had an interesting story to tell. He said I will let you find that out as you convey them to hospital. We surveyed the scene of this accident to find out what had happened. It appeared that a car had reversed out of a house into a service road over an embankment and then collided with a car on the main road. We placed the two patients from the car that had been hit, into our ambulance, they were suffering only with slight cuts and abrasions.

As we drove off towards St. Albans hospital they asked me which hospital they were going to. As I told them the look on their faces was disbelieving. I had to ask if there was a problem knowing that there was something going on and I wanted to hear the story that the fire officer already knew.

The woman confided to me 'Well, we are supposed to be working on a bus route in central London, I am a clippie and he's my driver, we are just going out for a quite drink together! We are going to have a problem explaining to our respective partners how we arrived at St.Albans'.

Now me being young and not really having been around long enough to impart any help to their predicament I said

'I am sure you will have enough time to come up with an answer'.

Have you been amazed how many people will drive around a puddle, and you nearly collide with them head on? The main road, between Berkhampstead and Ashridge, usually accidents involved deer running across the road without warning. This one involved a brand new car hitting another head on then colliding with an Ice cream van parked off the road. We conveyed three patients to hospital, the driver of the new car and the driver of the car he collided with. Unfortunately the new car driver's wife was killed outright. Whilst waiting for two more ambulance to arrive on the scene the police were asking the husband of the deceased for a quick statement of what had happened.

The man replied 'I have just picked up my new car and I saw a puddle on my side of the road so I drove around it!'

The policeman and I just looked at each other in amazement; he told the man that he would question him later on.

An accident on the A10 Ware viaduct, this incident had me thinking how this poor lorry driver must have thought as he went to his death.

I had a call very early one morning to a lorry that had gone off the Ware viaduct. and that a driver was trapped in his cab. I arrived on the top of the viaduct, because to gain access to the lorry by road, would have taken some time. Underneath was very marshy and flooded land and you would have to know the area very well to get near to the lorry. The fire service had set up a ladder from the top of the viaduct down to the overturned lorry I climbed down, which I think was about forty odd feet. Having got to the cab of the lorry the fire officer in charge told me he was already dead. I looked into the cab which was crushed onto the driver, he was still holding on to his steering wheel. I looked up to the road above from where he had come down from and could only think that this driver just knew this was going to be his last moments on earth. As he went through the crash barrier, braking hard, holding onto his steering wheel, and I can imagine his foot still slammed onto the brake peddle, as he sails through the air and overturns before slamming into the ground. I climbed back up to tell the ambulance crew that they were released and could return to their base. I found a police sergeant, and with the fire office in charge we discussed the best way we were going to get the driver out and away from the scene. It was agreed that the police would get their police surgeon to certify death and get undertakers to remove him to hospital once the fire service had recovered him from the cab.

This would take some time to get their rescue equipment to the lorry. I asked the sergeant what had happened, and it appeared that the lorry was travelling along in lane two of the dual carriageway when a woman pulled out into his lane without warning, causing him to brake hard and swerve to avoid colliding with the her he just went straight through the barrier without stopping.

The next day I could not understand why my legs were aching so much, then I realised it was the climb up and down that forty foot ladder.

Even now, as I travel over this viaduct I still think of the fate of this poor driver.

Off the A10 is a village called Barwick Ford and as the name suggest it contains a Ford. I was called to a car that had been swept away as it had attempted to cross the Ford. According my stepson Gary who came with me to take photos of the scene this was a notorious spot. Gary had himself been stuck in the middle of this Ford in his mini car and the water was rushing in through the door sills. Also he had come off his motor bike when going through it, he said that it was so slimly on the bottom of the ford that it could catch you unawares.

On our arrival the ambulance and three fire appliances were in attendance along with several senior fire officers and the police. It had been raining for several days and the water level had risen by several feet, and as the car attempted to cross the Ford it just got swept the away. The personnel from the emergency services spent several hours searching the river banks for the car with no luck. So apart from the police, we left the scene for the search to continue at first light.

The car was found the next morning over 200 hundred yards down the river with a female driver still in the car but unfortunately she was dead.

As I have said, any incident involving a baby or children is always a call I that attended apprehensively. Having received a call to St. Albans, to a group of school children being involved in a hit and run accident. I arrived with the ambulance and found a small group of young girls in hysterics, but about ten yards away there was a girl's body lying on the pavement. I walked swiftly over to her, and I stopped in my tracks, as I came across a brain lying in one piece about two yards from her. No wonder those poor girls were hysterical. I got a blanket from my car and lay it over the girl's body. I then went over to the group of girls to see if I could be of any help to the ambulance crew and the police who are now trying to pacify these girls. I got hold of one of the policemen to explain to him what had happened. I walked him over to the girl and prepared him to be as shocked as I was. I lifted the blanket to show him what had happened, even though I had prepared him he was still visibly shocked. All the girls' friends were put into police cars. The police took all their parents phone numbers and rung them to see if they wanted to come and collect their children or if they wanted the police to take them to their home addresses. It released us to move this poor girl into the ambulance and convey her to hospital for certification.

Before we left the scene the police had found out from the girl's what happened. The police explained to us that all the girls were waiting to cross the road to get on to a bus when a lorry came passed them carrying a portacabin. The load had protruded out over the width of the lorry, and the corner of the portakabin had hit the girl on the side of her head. The lorry driver would have been unaware that he had struck the girl as he carried on his journey. By the time we had all cleaned up at the hospital, after dealing with this child, the police arrived at the hospital they told us that they had traced the lorry and the driver. When they told him why he had been traced and stopped he was completely shocked. The police were awaiting the arrival of the girls parents who were being brought to the hospital, we gathered the girl was only twelve years old.

There were two further tragic accidents involving two small children which also upset me. The first one was in St.Albans where a three year old boy had been playing in the front garden of his house when his farther jumped into his car to reverse out of his drive and ran over his child and killed him instantly. Another was a three and half year old playing in a small street in Luton. The farther owned a tipper lorry, had called into his home before setting off again on his journey. As he reversed out of his small road he ran over his step child, and it was only other people that stopped him moving off from the scene as he was unaware what he had done.

In both these cases I could not even start to imagine how these farther's could possibly feel after these tragic accidents, I would think this will haunt them for the rest of their lives.

Between South Mimms and Potters Bar a car had collided with a tree and a driver reported trapped. While I was enroute, the dispatched ambulance had arrived on scene and the crew immediately asked if there was a Doctor on call who could attend the scene. I arrived to find a car had gone head on into a very large tree. Unfortunately large trees do not give. The impact had pushed the engine onto the driver's legs forcing them upwards into the steering wheel, which in turn had gone into his chest. He was in a very serious condition and to be perfectly honest I was amazed he was still alive. But the more incident I attended, the more I realised that when it's your turn to pass on into the next world it will only happen when it's your turn. Our on call doctor arrived on the scene had set up drip lines into the neck the only place which was assessable to him. The fire service took the car apart bit by bit, it was taking a long time to extricate the driver. The doctor turned around to us with a shocked look on his face, and said

'Look at this I've never seen anything like this in my life'

We look into car as the doctor pointed to the drivers groin area, the impact had ripped his trousers apart. On his thighs lay two testicals still attached to their seminal tract. The scrotum had split open through the impact. He also had fractures of both tibia's and fibula's and femurs, fractures of the both of arms, chest and spine. It took the fire service an hour to realise the driver from his car. He was taken into Barnett General Hospital, the doctor travelled to the hospital with the patient and I followed on to bring the doctor back to his car after he had handed the patient over to the waiting hospital medics.

CHAPTER 16:
Accidents

Accidents where do you stop? The list is endless, they can happen anywhere, in the home, work place, school and of course recreational.

While we were cleaning up our ambulance outside the casualty unit at St. Albans hospital a car rushed into ambulance parking area and a young lad jumped out shouting to us 'Can you give me a hand quickly please?'

We walked over to his car and saw another young male in a very shocked condition with a blood soaked towel wrapped around his hand and arm. While my crew mate went to fetch a chair to put him in, I asked what had happened to him. It appears that they had been in working their shed at home making fireworks, and whilst mixing the stuff together it had exploded causing serious injuries to his hand.

We took him into the causality unit and helped the nurse to take off the towel, the hand was in a complete mess. There were strands of flesh where a hand should have been. The doctors set to work to tidy up as best they could, asking me to get ready to convey him to Mount Vernon Plastics unit within twenty minutes.

Having got permission off our control we conveyed him to Mount Vernon for reconstructive surgery to his hand. A nurse came with us and was chatting away all the time to the young lad, in fact she took quite a shine to him. Some months later she told me she was going out with him, and some time after that they got married!

Gardening, is my wife's job apart from mowing the lawn that's a mans job,(Well I can dream) so when I attend a person reported burnt in his front garden I wondered what this person had been up to. We arrived at a house to see a man lying on the ground, as we got to him the fire brigade arrived. At the time there was a protocol that all fire related incidents had to be reported to the fire service, all the 999calls for an ambulance came into the joint control room so the fire service were never far behind us. I recognised the man straight away as he used to be in my class at school, he recognised me as well. Being black it did not help to see how burnt he was apart from his shirt sleeves on his arms were stuck to his skin and his face and hair were suffering from first degree burns. I asked him. 'What the hell have you been up to?'

'The grass was so long, I thought I ain't cutting that fucking lot, so I thought the best way, was setting light to it, so I poured petrol all over the grass and as I struck the match it just went whoosh!'

Well our class were not the brightest lot in the school! The casualty doctor and nurses had to smile at his misfortune. It was easy for me to have a laugh with him, because he was the kind of lad at school who was always playing pranks on someone, he was always very good humoured. After leaving school he had set up a very successful pop band. I was also pleased that the casualty doctor also had a job in assessing his burns of the colour of his skin, because I thought it was just me.

We transferred him to Mount Vernon Burns unit for treatment; he was assessed as having received 24% burns to his arms and face of first and second degree burns.

There are quite a few Farms in our and we don't go to them that often and finding them when called is not an easy job no maps no sat nav in those days. So early one morning having just come on duty at 0700 hrs, we were called out to a man attacked by a pig! We hadn't even had time to check our vehicle, but in those days we always relied on each other as we were handed over from the other crew that the ambulances would be fully stocked, clean and ready to go. Off we went to this isolated farm some nine miles away in Markyate, just on the Bedfordshire borders. Going down narrow lanes stopping every now again to check if the name of the farm was the one we wanted. We came to it on a bend, then up a narrow unmade track into the area of the pig sty's.

A man presented himself to us who announced he was the farmer, he told us that his pigman had been attacked by a sow whilst he was in the pen. The pigman had been in the sty and he was trying to get to the sows piglets, to sex them. Then he was going to castrate the boys! In normal circumstances he went on to tell us that the sow then eats the testicals that have been cut out of these poor little boys. Things you learn, but more seriously, was the sow still in with the patient who was in the pen, thank goodness no. He had the most serious injury to his leg I had seen to that day. His left thigh had been bitten right down to the femur just leaving a big hole! The farmer had a laid back approach to us, as he had been telling the history of how his pigman had got his injury, this caught me unawares. Because of the trauma the body had shut down, and there was very little blood. The only sensibly thing we could use to cover the wound was a pillow case! loaded him onto our ambulance and rush him into Luton & Dunstable hospital. Informing control to alert and to have a doctor standing bye. In those days we did not have all the equipment to tell us his blood pressure etc, but could tell by his skin tone and his shallow breathing that he was in severe shock. His age was against him as well as he was over seventy years of age. We arrived, rushed him into causality now in a very bad way, the doctors got to work on him straight away. They could not believe the injury that he had sustained either, as more doctors came to assist. Every one involved said they had never seen such a serious injury to a patient who was still alive, having given all the conditions that had been presented. I never heard any more about the patient's condition, but I know that if he had died we would have been asked by the police for a statement for the coroner.

I learnt a lot about pigs that day and I will make sure I don't meet up with a sow and her piglets. I felt for those poor little piglet boys though, it made my eyes water as the farmer explained how the little boys lost their manhood. You get a razor blade, a ball of cotton and some Dettol, then just find the balls and nick them out! And dab the area with Dettol! The twinge I felt between my legs as he explained it

Very young children and water do not mix. I had just sat down to eat my lunch, when a call came in to go to a large house in St. Albans to a child in a pond. We raced to the scene, arrived within four minutes to find a very annoyed mother cursing us, in taken so long to arrive. I took the child from the mother, which was limp and life less. I started mouth to mouth immediately and jumped into the ambulance without stopping. My crew mate knew we just had to go like hell and tell control we were going straight to the recovery ward at St. Albans. Enroute I was still doing mouth to mouth and cardiac compressions. We had the choice in those days that if a patient was in a serious condition we could by pass the casualty department and go straight into the recovery department which was adjacent to the operating theatres which would have all the anaesthetist and surgeons there immediately. We arrived at the hospital, and I ran off down the corridor with this small child in my arms and the mother still shouting at me to keep the child's head up. The doctors took over immediately as I explained that the mother had told me that her little boy of two had walked off into the garden and fallen into the gold fish pond where she found him. She was unaware how long he had been in the pond. We stayed with the team working on this poor little boy until the doctors called it time to pronounce death. When I checked the time for my paper work, we had been in the hospital for nearly an hour. Children's deaths are to me and all my work colleagues very sad and very upsetting occasions!

Lightning strikes on people, I had heard over the radio a number of times over the years, but this my first occasion of attending such an incident. I was on call when I was called to children and adults who had been struck by lightning whilst playing football. Control having assessed the information had initially responded by sending four ambulances to this incident. I knew the area well as I was brought up not far from this location which was a small wooded area with an opening in it which was just big enough to have a kick about in.

The first ambulance managed to gain access in to the area but over hanging branches, knocked off the offside blue light, and

241

on the way back out, knocked the other one off! Unfortunately that was the least of their problems because we had ten patients to deal with. A group of dads and their boys were just having fun on a "Sunday" afternoon playing football, coats as goal posts and enjoying themselves.

They told us it started to rain and almost immediately there was thunder and lightning, so they all ran for cover under some very large tress when the lightning struck one of the trees knocking to the floor ten people. Four patients that had been leaning against the tree suffered burns and cardiac arrest. The other six suffered after being thrown to the ground and being knocked unconscious, also causing some heart problems from the massive electric force as it went down the tree into the ground. I had another officer at the scene to assist with triage and helping others in gaining access to this clearing in the woods with the vehicles. The most seriously injured were taken to St. Albans city hospital which was only a mile and half from the incident. The less seriously injured were conveyed to Hemel Hempstead Hospital. We had five ambulances to convey these patients to hospital, unfortunately two children died and one adult had serious burns and heart problems.

Publicans! Now you would think that these men would be able to serve behind a bar and know when the cellar door is open. Well the answer is a big NO. I had to attend two different pubs where, so the landlords said they were so busy serving the customer they forgot the cellar door was open and fell in! In one of those cases falling twelve feet into the cellar. Both publicans had broken arms and broken legs and were quite seriously injured. Also in both cases we had to have the assistance of another ambulance crew as well as the fire service. The good thing about the fire service is they have ropes and know how to do knots and they come in fives and have bigger muscles than I have. With all this help we soon managed these rescues. We first had to place them on our special rescue stretcher, the paraguard, then up to ground level, through the bar so we could get them into the ambulance with out causing more injury. On one of these occasions I remembered some one saying, as we carried the publicans out of the pub, 'You must be drinking stronger beer than you are serving us George!'

This went down like a "Lead Balloon".

"Ladders"! another accident black spot. My wife hates me going up ladders its only because I am not insured enough for her at the moment. I have lost count as to how many I have been called to, too many to mention. Ones I recall a steeple jack working on a church spire. He fell from his ladder some thirty feet, before hitting the wooden base at the start of his ladders, which was still another 30feet from the ground. He suffered from serious spinal and head injuries. Two days later we had to convey him under police escort to Stoke Mandeville Hospital in Aylesbury.

The reason for the police escort we needed a slow steady ride with no stopping, also keeping the ambulance in the centre of the road to avoid as many drain covers and holes in the road. These escorts were carried out by motor cyclist and were very good in keeping us moving.

Without listening to his wife's objections a man who falls off his ladder, he had gone to the rescue of a squirrel, that had got stuck in the gutter of his house.. He got up the ladder and as he got hold of the squirrel it bit him! This caused him to pull his hand away and lose his balance and fall to the ground! He ended up with a fracture to the skull, fracture of the spine and fracture of his pelvis. Worst of all was the abuse he received from his wife for going up there in the first place!

'I told the silly old sod he's 73 not to go up the bloody ladder would he listen,

No because he's a man, your all bloody stubborn' she said

Not much sympathy there then I thought as we loaded him into the ambulance!

A small village in Breachwood Green near Luton airport, not the easiest of villages to get to, I was on call and the nearest for providing medical aid for some little while. I knew as I soon as got near to the address that this was going to be fatal because there was a group of people standing outside of a brick wall to the garden of the house. I got out of my car and these people just pointed to inside the wall where I found a male deceased and a ladder on top of him. Having been to several incidents like this I was surprised to find him dead as most people manage some how to slide with the ladder and come away with serious injuries but never the less recoverable ones. He was only in his forties and apparently a very fit man, but unfortunately what ever went wrong with his ladder had caught him unawares , and unable to do anything about it.

Recreational accidents. This is another endless list of football and rugby incidents that stretch us to breaking point at weekends, especially on a Sunday. Call after call come into control calling for an ambulance for broken legs, arms, facial injuries and thankfully not that often but one is to often a fracture of the spine mainly to rugby players. I can think of endless occasions when the crews try to get the ambulance as near to the patient as possible, when the ambulance gets bogged down on the pitch and has to be pushed and pulled to get back off the muddy ground with the help and assistance of the rest of the players and spectators.

One very unusual recreational accident was to a sports hall in Potters Bar. The crew on scene had called for the assistance of another crew and the fire service. As they didn't have a crew to send for some time so I was sent. A twelve year old girl who had been training on a trampoline had fallen on to her hands causing both wrist to break (Collis fracture) This was such an unusual incident we could only use entonox on this girl. With the assistance of the fire service we placed her onto a paraguard stretcher. I must admit I had never been near a trampoline before and was surprised at how high off the ground they are, and even moving very slowly how springy they are. Bit by bit we edged her to the edge of the trampoline where the fire service had placed ladders and we slid her to the ground. It was surprisingly a very difficult job. Just as we got her into the ambulance the mother of the girl turned up, she told us that her daughter had only started training that night having just got over one fracture of the wrist six months ago!

A Bee keeper decided as he had been keeping bees for years he didn't need to wear his protective clothing apart from head gear. The call was to a man stung by bees! While on route my colleague and I were discussing how we were going to get near the man if the bees were still around him. We would not have long to find out as the call was not that far from our station. On our arrival we were met by another bee keeper who had managed to clear the bees away from this man. He told us that they had been collecting honey when this swarm of bees suddenly appeared and attacked his friend. Our patient had only been wearing shorts and a short sleeve shirt! He had been stung over the whole of his body; we rushed him into hospital which was less than five minutes away.

We went back later in the day to see how he had got on and the sister said it was one of the most time consuming jobs she had ever under taken, she and the doctor removed well over two hundred bee stings out of this mans body.

Two brothers went shooting pigeons on a farm just outside Luton. While they were sitting behind their straw bails hiding from the bird's one of the brothers double barrel gun went off, which was lying across his lap shooting his brother full blast in the leg. The only reason I was called to this incident was that I had a Vauxhall Frontera 4x4 and it was going to be the only way to get an ambulance to him as he was in the middle of field. When I arrived crew had walked about half mile into this field to this injured man. They had set up two drip lines into the patient, We placed him into my fully equipped vehicle which also had a stretcher and rushed him off to the Luton & Dunstable hospital. Unfortunately the patient had to have his leg amputated as the damage caused by shooting was far too great to save it.

About four months later the patient rung me up and asked if he could come and meet up with the crew who had attended the scene, to say thank you to us. He duly turned up on a motor bike with a side car attached. He explained it's the only way he can get about, because he can't keep his balance on the motor bike on its own. Whilst he had a temporary artificial limb he was not confident yet to take the weight of the bike in case he forgot and put the wrong leg down first as some times it feels its still there. He told us how the accident had happened, his brother's gun, unknown to his brother had a faulty safety catch and had failed to engage. As he placed the gun onto his lap to rest, the gun went off blasting him with both barrels. The reason he had come to see us was because he had been told by the surgeons at L&D that the paramedics had saved his life in their swift action in setting up two lines which in those days was a revolution. It was a great influence and satisfaction to crews to see that all their hard work, training and late nights in studying for their exams to become paramedics had paid off in saving lives.

Once again a Sunday afternoon,(Its like the Boom Town rats I Hate Mondays Song) to Hemel Hempstead this time to four people having been burnt by an explosion. I arrived just as the third ambulance was arriving in a road which was full of fire and police vehicles as well as ambulances. I gathered from the crews on scene that these people were having a BBQ and that it had exploded. We conveyed all four adults to hospital one adult male suffering from 80% burns one female 70% burns, one male with 10% burns to his legs and one female with very minor burns but in severe shock.

We stood by at the hospital, knowing that we would have to transfer them to the burns unit at Mount Vernon hospital. We learnt how this incident happened from the severely shocked young female. It transpired that the young male with the 10% burns to his legs was her fiancé and he had come around to see his future Mother and Farther in law and to cook them a BBQ. The BBQ was not lighting quickly enough for him, so he got a can of petrol and as he poured it onto the coals it set light to the can, He instinctively threw it over his head and shoulders backwards. Unfortunately his futures in law were sitting behind him with their daughter! The petrol was sprayed all over them and as it was still alight, this is what had caused the serious burns to them all.

When you are accessing burns to see if the victims are going have a successfully outcome from their injuries, you add the percentage of burns to the age of the victim and the nearer you get to 100 the more likely it is that it will end in the death of the person. As these two people were in their fifties the 100 rule had been surpassed for any successful outcome for them. Even so the burns unit at Mount Vernon were willing to take all three patients and so we loaded up three ambulances, under police escort and transferred them to the burns unit.

Unfortunately we learnt later that the father and mother died later in the week,

I had two calls to my own town of Harpenden. The first call was to an elderly female on fire in a Nursing Home! On my arrival I found a very confused and panicky staff in this home shouting at me to hurry up to get into a small bedroom were an elderly lady was sitting in chair with slight burns to her mouth and nose. I asked what had happened and the only explanation that was forth coming from the carerars was that the lady has piped oxygen through a nasal tube, it was thought she had lit up a cigarette. Flames and oxygen are a lethal combination. Whilst the burns were not significant on her face the inside of her mouth and airway were black from the flash burns. A crew arrived and with out further ado she was rushed off to hospital. The police and fire service were in attendance and I told the police woman that this was likely to prove fatal to the lady and she ought to get the ball rolling informing her sergeant etc. She was some what surprised at this, so I had to explain, that whilst the outside of her face was only slightly burnt the inside of her mouth and airway would be swelling up as the ambulance was on route to the hospital now, and she could be dead within a few hours. I was unfortunately right, she died within six hours of being admitted into hospital.

The second incident involved a thirteen year old boy who had been electrocuted whilst on a bridge overlooking a railway line. This location was down a very narrow lane and the nearest house was about 200yds away. On my arrival there were several young lads and an adult who had called the ambulance from the nearby house. A boy was lying on his back, he was in cardiac arrest, so I started mouth to mouth and cardiac compressions. The boy's friends told me what had happened; he had been electrocuted by hanging over the bridge with a fishing rod which touched the overhead cables to the trains. I got a slight pulse but it went again, but I kept working until a crew arrived. We loaded him on the ambulance straight away and I travelled in the ambulance maintaining cardiac massage whilst enroute to the hospital. On arrival at the hospital doctors and nursing staff were waiting for us, but after working on him for forty minutes the doctors called time.

We had to go back to the scene of the incident to pick up my car and tidy up my equipment. We were met by the police, they told us what had happened. The group of boys had got a fishing rod and had been dangling it over the bridge taken it in turns. Our thirteen year old was unfortunately the one that got near enough to the cables. The police were having problems in tracing the parents as they were not at home, what a trauma for them to come home to.

"Sunday" morning we were called to a man with back injury. We found a man in a very distressed condition bent over unable to move, his back had just locked up. The other problem was, as he had been bent over for some time he was having difficulty in breathing. His wife said he always got up at seven thirty to make a cup of tea and then come back to bed. As he hadn't come back to bed by eight fifteen she got up to find out why he had still not brought up the tea. She was surprised to find him in his condition on the door step.

We didn't have entonox or any other pain killers in those days, so we decided the only way we could move him was to lay him onto the ground on his side, as he could not be straighten up. Once he was lying down his breathing started to settle down. He told us that as he went to pick up the milk off the step, he felt his back just go ping and a burning sensation went all up his legs and back, he said he couldn't even fall to the ground. Being bent over he couldn't even shout for help to his wife. With assistance of another crew we got him into the ambulance and off to hospital for treatment. His wife had to make her own cup of tea, before she made her way to the hospital!

Us ambulance bods should know better you think, well not to one of my officer colleagues. As he was doing a bit of DIY in his house, one weekend, he drilled through a water pipe in the wall of his kitchen. The reason I got called, was he also electrocuted himself as well. Off I went to his house to find him in the back of the ambulance about to go off to hospital, with slight burns to his hand and still laughing as he told me what had happened to him. He was putting up a shelve in his kitchen and drilled through his cold water pipe, as he put his finger in the hole to stem the flow of water, the water sprayed into his drill causing him to get a electric shock and to fall off his step ladder! Just shows if you need a job done don't get ambulance officer to do it.

DIY it's alright if read the instruction on the tin, and being men we don't need to do that easy stuff. As we go to a man unconscious in his kitchen. As we entered the kitchen there was such a strong smell of glue, and a male deeply unconscious. The kitchen floor was half laid with tiles and a big tin of glue was there. We ascertained he was not on any medication or suffered from fits, and he was normally fit and well. We moved him out side into the fresh air and he started to come round from his unconscious state. The only conclusion we came to for his illness was that he had been working in such a confined space with the doors and widows shut that he had been overcome by the fumes from the glue. After a short time in hospital for a check up he was allowed to go home and finish his handy work. Hopefully with the doors and widows open like it said on the tin!

Now the following three calls could be accidents in the home or recreational I will let the reader decide! But beware.

St.Albans ambulance had a call from control to a male who had fallen down stairs with serious injuries. We asked control what the injuries were but the caller would not say, only that it was serious. So we duly turned up, to find the door was open, we walked in, to find a male naked apart from a towel clutched to his groin. We asked what has happened, and he replied that whilst vacuum cleaning the house he had slipped on the stairs and the beater part of the Hoover had severely damaged his manhood! We asked if we could remove the towel so we could examine the said area, he was correct, he had nearly decimated his penis.

'Were you naked doing your house work' my colleague asked

'Yes' came the reply

'You say you fell down the stairs, have you hurt yourself any where else?'

'No should I have' he replied indignantly

'Possible but not to worry'

We can only assume that the brushes to the hover had taken most of his penis into it. We found the Hoover and whilst all the brushes were covered in blood there was no point in looking into the bag as any tissue we would have recovered would have been too badly damaged and contaminated to be of use for grafting. We later took him to Mount Vernon hospital for plastic surgery. And we knew he had been masturbating himself with the Hoover, as we have heard of three others cases in Hertfordshire

Attending to a call in a hotel in Hemel Hempstead one Saturday night, and as Hemel ambulances were busy, we trundled off to a man having problems with his water works! So our witty reply to control was that he should have called a plumber not us. They did not appreciate our humour!

On our arrival at the Hotel the patient was already standing outside the hotel awaiting our arrival. I got out of the ambulance to go to open the rear doors of the ambulance and the patient came towards me. 'What's the problem?' I ask

'Well', he said 'I am a bit embarrassed, as you can hear I am an American'

'Don't worry' I said 'I wont hold that against you',

Trying to be helpful and he grimly smiled back at me.

'I had these two girls in my room and they well, um, how can. I say, um, they had this party trick'

I am now hooked on every word he says.

'They have put a ring thing on my down below! Um, well, um, I have an erection that won't go down and I thought you boys would know what to do'

It was my turn to go 'um, ah, well the best thing we can do is take you into hospital for them to sort out'

I told him, the reason the erection stayed in place, the ring was stopping the blood flow back into his body in simplistic terms. He said thank you and off we went to casualty.

It was the first week in August, when new doctors take over in hospital. We handed him over to the sister, who called the doctor straight over. The doctor was a young new doctor who coloured up and asked the sister what she should do. The sister said that she would have to call the fire service to get a ring cutter.

'Oh my god' The doctor said

'They never told me about these things when we went through medical school' The fire service turned up and the doctor duly carried out the necessary operation to the offending mans ring!

Three weeks later we are called once again to the same Hotel. This time to a man who was constipated! "So why call us?" we asked control, they told us he was a holiday maker and had no GP. We arrived, and once again we are met at the front of the hotel by the patient. This time it's a Canadian who has called us, I opened the back doors to the ambulance and he walked knocked kneed into the ambulance. I told him to have a seat and tell me what the problem was.

'I had better not' He replies, 'I can't sit down I am on holiday from overseas and one of the girls I am with, has lost a dildo in my arse!'

I couldn't help it but I had to say 'Well its not actually lost, its temporary out of reach'.

That also went down like a lead balloon. Off we went to hospital and low and behold the same doctor is on.

'I don't believe it, your doing this to me on purpose'

'Oh by the way' I said, and told her what the patient had told me,

'And it's still vibrating!' I said smiling as I left

We left her to it, as we went on merry way back to base. Saying how do these foreigners know about this Hotel, and it's going on's and we don't.

In all these three cases, it brought tears to our eyes, and a big bit of inward breathing.

A new estate was being built in London Colney and for the period it was a revolutionary way of building, it was being mainly of wood. There had been a salesman demonstrating a new piece of equipment for most of the morning to the builders. It was nail gun, and his party piece at the end of his talk was a demo, to hold it up to the side of his face and pull the trigger! This was to demonstrate how safe the gun was, as it had to be placed against a hard surface to be able to fire the nail into wood. That was ok until he got to the fourth demo, he pulled the trigger and bang, it goes off blowing most of his bottom jaw apart!

He ended up going to Mount Venom hospital for plastic surgery. The dental surgeon he was under was also my dentist at the Royal Free hospital. I was able to ask how he was progressing. He said it was the first time he had, had to do so much reconstruction, for some considerable time. He went on to say, he thought the last time, he had done so much surgery on a jaw and teeth reconstruction, was when he was dealing with soldiers, who had been in combat zones.

Now guards are put machines for a reason not for this man, trapped in machinery. The fire service station is within minutes from this printing firm. On our arrival the fire service were hard at work trying to release the man from the printing machine. He had tried to reach into the machine without stopping it to retrieve a sheet of paper that had got jammed in the rollers. As he freed the paper the machine dragged his arm up to his shoulder before the machine stopped. The fire officer said that it was going to take at least half an hour or more to take the machine apart.

I was called to go to Luton & Dunstable hospital to pick up a medical team, consisting of a doctor and the A&E sister. I conveyed them to the scene the doctor got to work straight away and gave the patient morphine and put another line of Hartmans into him. The fire service managed to release the patient. The patient arm had gone between four sets of rollers designed to take only the thickness of paper. Every bone from the fingers all the way to the shoulder was fractured. I never did find out how the patient progressed in hospital.

CHAPTER 17:
Keep it in the Family

Having joined the service in 1964 my next big move was to meet up with a nurse and we married in the 1965, her name was Terri. We rented a room some away from our work. We used to cycle to work and when we were on opposing shifts the only time we met up was when we passed each other on the road. One day it was so foggy we missed each other!

Then in 1966 my son Andrew was born, the year England won the world cup.

As I sitting in the waiting room of the maternity unit at QE11 hospital talking to another expectant farther, in walks the sister and shouts out

'Who is Mr Enstone'

I raise my hand 'Me' clearing my throat and the same time.

'You have a son he's only got one ear! Speak to you later'

All this was done, without stopping, looking me in the face, she walked in and turned all at the same time as she spoke all those words.

I looked at the bloke opposite me in total disbelief at what happened here, I thought I was dreaming. The man said 'What the fuck was that all about'

'I've no idea' as I got up in shock and walked out of the room to find some one to talk to. I didn't for over 40 minutes. And I can assure you I was not a happy bunny the way I was treated.

This little bundle, turned out to be the biggest trouble maker in the family ever since that day!

In 1970 my daughter Nicola was born, keeping Haemophilia in the Family.

I have a mild form of Factor V111(10%), so my daughter had to be a carrier as that's how this gene carries on through the generations. But as with all things in our strange family she is also affected and has a low factor V111 as well!

Having divorced Terri, I marry my second wife Valerie. She had three boys of her own Paul and twins Gary and Michael, Her first husband having died following a heart attack

So going back to my bundle of trouble Andrew, when he was only nine months old, he was involved in his first RTA! I was in bed after a night shift and my wife had taken Andrew out in the pram into the village of Redbourn where we lived, and as she was crossing the road on a Zebra crossing, a car overtook the cars that had stopped to let them cross, and careered into them, pulling the pram out of the grip of my wife, throwing Andrew out of the pram. Luckily the pram was a big Silver Cross, it was severely damaged. As it was a cold day Andrew was wrapped up in several blankets, he was found in the gutter by people who witnessed the accident. One of the shopkeepers came running up to my house knocking on my door to wake me up to tell me what had happened. Off to hospital we went to have Andrew and Terri checked over but it wasn't until a week later that Andrews's leg was diagnosed with a greenstick fracture.

We had made such a fuss as he was not being able to put his foot down and kept lifting it up like a dog would. The Paediatric Consultant who lived in the Village got to hear about our complaint and checked Andrew himself, and it was him who diagnosed the fracture ,the casualty doctor had missed.

The police informed us later that the cars brakes had failed, and that's why he overtook the cars in front of him but could not avoid hitting the pram. As the village bobby said, it was very lucky that Andrew was in this big pram because he would hate to think what the outcome would have been otherwise.

The next call for Andrew to be hospitalized was when he fell over in his class room hitting his head on the desk knocking him out. My wife was called to take him to hospital! I was on 9 to 5 shift, and in London, so when I got back into the area I was told to phone up control from St. Albans hospital, and they told me that my wife had rung them to tell me that Andrew had been admitted to St.Albans children's ward.

It just goes on and on with another accident at Senior school this time, playing football he pulled his cruciate ligament, I was at home this time and I conveyed him straight to RNO hospital at

Stanmore which was the best orthopaedic hospital around, it also had a Casualty unit at the time

A Firework Display at Watford Football where I was the Incident Ambulance officer, in case of a medical need. That night we needed three ambulances because a rocket from the display went off course and shot into the crowd, injuring six people that we had to convey to hospital. These fireworks had just missed my wife Val, Andrew and his girl friend. Ah I he got away with it this time, but no, driving out of Watford town, control called me up to say they have a call to an RTA in Watford believed to be your son involved. Sure enough it was, he had been waiting at a set of traffic lights, a car rammed into him causing him to crash into the car in front. Neither doors, off his XR2 would not open, so he had to climb out, through, the sunshine roof. Luckily he and girlfriend them were not injured so I took them home. This was his second XR2, that he had owned and both of them had been involved in an accident, and both had to be written off.

I hoped that was going to be last time I got called to him in his cars, well it was.

Because next time it was another football accident, playing five aside football at the right old age of twenty nine. He goes and breaks his Tibia & Fibula, it was a very bad break. My daughter Nicola was at our house as it was Fathers Day. We went off to the hospital, to meet up with the crew who had conveyed him to hospital, they warned me how bad the break was. His leg took sometime to heal, and to get sorted out. I was not impressed with the doctors at the hospital and said so.

Val, rang me one day whilst at work which was quite unusual, to say she had been attacked at home by some male person. Without hesitation I was enroute to our home from office in Luton and on my arrival, there was an ambulance just down the road from the house and two police cars, with every one hanging on to a male person. The police shouted at me 'We are here not up there'

'Right I will be with you soon'

I went into my house to find my wife. She told me what had happened to her. She had seen a man sitting on our front wall with blood on his head, the next thing she knew was this man bashes down our side gate. He walks in through the patio window which was slightly open to let the newly plastered walls dry out. She gets hold of him and pushes him through the house and out the front door receiving a smack in her face for her troubles.

I said to her I would be back in a minute while I went to see this bloke. I got to the police and ambulance crew who asked where the hell I had been. They were still fighting with this man, in the end it took seven of us to restrain him and place him into the ambulance. I told one of the policemen

'I been to see my wife, as she was attacked by this man'.

'Oh sorry we have been chasing this bloke for over half an hour, he has committed six attacks on people so far, before we caught up with him I didn't know about your wife'

I took a look at this young man and could tell he was on some kind of drug. He was still fighting in the ambulance even though he was handcuffed and being sat upon whilst they took him off to hospital with his head wound. We didn't want him to injure himself anymore than he had already, because it would have meant too much paper work.

It turned out that he had taken LSD, an illegal drug that can cause severe hallucinations and paranoia. He had knocked down and broken a wooden front door on one house, assaulted a girl, pulled a van driver out of his van, attacked an elderly couple in their home and then my wife before being caught by the police. They had been chasing him from one call to the next. As it had been snowing all morning they just followed the blood trail.

Unbeknown to us it all went to court and he got a fine and community service. He appealed against his very light sentence and at the appeal, as the CPS (Crown Prosecution Service) had not got all the evidence at the time the judge threw out the case and he was let off!, **Disgusting.**

We had to have a new side gate and the carpets from the dining room where he entered through the kitchen and hallway all cleaned as he left a trail of blood behind him.

My granddad even got into the act, I was going on duty at 1500 at St. Albans station when he asked if he could have a lift up to the town because it was Armistice Day, he wanted to parade through the town, having served in the Royal Navy in the First World War. Now my Grandma said he's a silly old fool going up there at his age

(He was 80 at the time and at 84 he was still riding my brothers Claude Butler racing bike!) I told him no problem granddad and as I dropped him off I asked how he was going to get back home he said

'Don't worry that far ahead lets get there first.'

He was a great old man and lived until he was 103, During the whole of the time I knew him, having lived with my mum and grandparents for 14 years, I never heard him raise his voice, lose his temper or worry about any thing, and not one single swear word did I hear him utter. Having dropped him off I went into work and as it was a Sunday (again) I and the other crew members used to sit in the control room and watch, all the other crews working whilst we sat there. A call came in from the police, could we attend St.Albans Abbey at the front entrance to a male fallen, immediately I said

'That's my bloody granddad, my grandma will be furious'.

Yes, I was right we got to the front entrance and my granddad was propped up against the door of the Abbey and he had broken his patella. The first words he said

'I thought it might be you, I don't have to worry about getting home now do I'

I said 'I just knew it would be you as well what's grandma going say to you?'

'I don't know, you listen to her for me!'

He was a truly great old man with a very dry sense of humour.

The next time I took granddad into hospital was when he was 100 years old and the Chinese doctor was delighted to meet such an old man, as the Chinese believe it brings them good luck, when they meet up with someone of that age. He was treated as if he was a King, and the doctor listened to him intently as he talked about his Maritime adventures and his life.

So that only leaves my daughter Nicola, and she was just as bad in getting injured! At the age of ten she went out with my son to walk the dog one evening, she promptly slipped on some mud and falls and breaks her wrist! So I rung up the Royal Free hospital, that she and I are both under and get some smart arse doctor. As I explained to him that my daughter had a Collis fracture, to which he asked and where is that? So I told him in no uncertain terms not to treat people as morons, and if he wasn't sure go and look it up, and the clue is, it wasn't in the leg. On arrival at the hospital I met up with this doctor who was more than sheepish to say the least, and luckily for him, the senior doctor from the haemophilia department was there and said

'I have been told by my colleague that you told him to go and find out what a Collis fracture was, because you wouldn't give him a clue!'

'Oh I gave him a clue alright, and he was lucky I could have said more'

I could see he was laughing, because he knew what I did for a living, and I had been going to this hospital for years and he knew my sense of humour. She was to be kept in for the night after the "op" on her wrist had been carried out. We went up into the ward with her to be told by the sister you have no need to worry. we are all highly trained on this ward and your daughter will be well looked after. Why she said that I don't know, I wasn't worried at all, it was a simple fracture and apart from the blood clotting problem she had she would get over it fine.

Imagine my surprise when I turn up early next morning, with both arms held up by bandages on drip stands, with a plate of food in front of her. This consisted of a boiled egg and two slices of bread. I was dumb struck to say the least. I walked straight round to the sister desk to say to her.

'Your staff might be highly trained but they have no common sense'

'Er why what's the matter Mr Enstone?' she asked.

I asked her to come and see Nicola and see the problem herself. It took her a good twenty seconds to see that Nicola had no use of her arms, and that the food had been placed there without any thought of how she was going to eat it.

Clearing her throat 'I understand, Mr Enstone, the problem here I will get onto it straight away'

'Don't bother I will do it, now I am here, but please ensure your clever nursing staff never leave a child looking at food again, because they are unable to feed themselves.'

She went off with her tail between her legs.

Like her brother the next two calls that came in from control were

'Hello Mr Enstone it's to inform you that your daughter has been picked up from an RTA in Bricket Wood and is enroute to St. Albans hospital with minor injuries'

So off I go, and meet up with her at the hospital. Gerry had taken her in to hospital and he had known my daughter from a baby. He gave me a broad grin as I arrived,

'Nicola has taken over from Andrew in the accident stakes'

She had been standing on the pavement with her friends when this young lad driving a car saw them, pulled up to talk to them but didn't realise how fast he was going and ploughed into them. Apart from bruising she was fine.

The phone rings 'Hello Mr Enstone, just to let you know that your daughter has been involved in an RTA in London Colney High Street.'

Says the cheerful control manager. 'Hadn't she just had an accident a couple of weeks ago?'

'Well funny you should say that, it would be easy to say when doesn't she have one' I replied

This time she was waiting to turn right in her car when some bloke decides he wanted to modify two cars, my daughters and his! The usual thing from the motorist, I never saw you there where did you come from? My daughter who is not a wallflower by any means replies 'I can't come from any where, you moron you hit me in the back'

She was carted off to hospital, by, yes you guessed Gerry again.

He said 'I am becoming your personal bloody medic and I am going to ask for more money'

'Well you can ask, but I think you know what the answer might be'

'Bloody officers you are all the same, no, to everything'

She only received whiplash this time, other wise she was ok apart from being upset over her little car being damaged beyond repair.

Oh, and just going back to my wife, she had not been well and I thought it could be Meningitis. I called our GP who came around within 20 minutes. He was not sure what was going on, as there was a rash when I called him, but it had gone by the time he arrived. She had the signs and symptoms of Meningitis, but he was not certain and said to keep my eye on her during the night, ring me if things change. She had a terrible night, so I rang at 0600 and he was there with in 20 minutes again. Right lets get an ambulance for her and get her into hospital. I contacted control and an ambulance was sent straight away. We arrive at Hemel Hempstead hospital where she under went a lumber puncture and sure enough she had meningitis!

It's lucky I am the only sane, healthy person, no grey hairs and upright, in my family! And if you believe that stop reading this book now.

CHAPTER 18:
Police and Fire

As I have already said the working relationship with the police, has from my point of view been a great success. The Fire service relationship has been quite fraught at times to say the least.

Some of the thing we used to get away with in the old days would be seen as not P.C. or somewhat not cricket. I have known fireman come back from lorry accidents loaded with items that got in the way when dealing with an entrapment or a Fire!

A lorry carrying Salmon from Scotland turned over at London Colney roundabout. The driver was trapped for an hour before being rescued from his cab. Some how, some of those little fishes managed to swim out of the rear of the lorry into the fire appliances! But we all enjoyed some nice salmon steaks for a couple of days after that, especially when in those days it was a luxury item, which made it taste better still.

Two fires, involving HGV, brought more stock for the canteen. One containing

Potatoes, and the other one sugar, those were the days!

I attended a house fire in St. Albans where it was reported that persons were trapped and we arrived prior the fire appliances. The house was well alight on our arrival, the street is a small and there were loads of onlookers, and one family was shouting at us, to get into the house because there were people and children still in the house. The hallway was full of paraffin heaters and plastic bottles of paraffin even on top of the heaters. I rushed into a back room looking for anyone in there. I searched down stairs and found no one. Then the firemen came in with their breathing apparatus on, I went back out into the street for fresh air, then went back into the house again. This time I went upstairs and searched as best as I could, as we had been informed a small child was missing. My lungs now were getting full up of smoke so I have to give up, and go back down stairs, to the ambulance and have a breather. The fire service was still searching the premises when the Divisional fire officer arrived and asked what was going on. I told him that I had been inside the house to look for this missing child with no luck. He now goes into the house and within minutes he rushes out of the house with this child in his arms, and hands him over to us and tells us to go now. We rush of to the hospital and arrived within minutes and handed the child over to the doctors that were standing by for arrival. They tried to resuscitate the little boy but after forty five minutes they had to give up and pronounce his death.

I called up control, who told me to return to the station where the Divisional fire officer wanted to see me. I walked into his office which is on the second floor and he told me to sit down. He then proceeded to tell me, he had found the child in bedroom under the bed, which you had searched, he emphasised this statement

'Why didn't you find him before I did?'

Before I could answer he went to on say

'I tell you why, because you never looked properly, people hide in very strange places when they are scared. So the next time you go rushing into a house look in places you normally would not look into'

He never stopped talking in a very harsh voice,

'If you had found this little boy sooner you might have saved his life, instead his parents are having to arrange a funeral. It should not be left up to me to come some time later to do what you should have done.'

This took me by complete surprise, I was not expecting a pat on the back by any means but I didn't expect this torrid load of abuse and crap he was coming out with. As he went to go on with more I stepped in and said

'Excuse me **SIR** but your teams were in there as well, and they also had B/A (Breathing Apparatus), so why I am the one being pulled up here, also I am not trained in fire fighting, and its because we arrived prior to your machines I felt it was my place to go in there to try my best to find anyone. As I went down the hallway I managed to push two people who were in the house out, before they became in danger from the fire. I don't feel this is right, you are attacking me and I am leaving you to rant on at your desk,'

I stormed out of his office. My colleague and the control room officers who I went to see after this incident were amazed that he had spoken to me like, but that's what I found that some fire officers they were bullies.

The fire service would always call us to a scene of a large fire even if there were no reports of any injuries, it was a protocol they had in case any of their personnel were injured whilst they were fighting the fire.

One very hot afternoon a Homebase store caught fire in St.Albans, whilst all the staff and customers were safely evacuated, we stood by in case any firemen were injured. We had to deal with firemen exhausted from the heat of the fire and the hot weather. I was unable to get access to cold drinking water for the firemen, but I noticed just around the corner from the fire there was a warehouse belonging to Schweppes, the soft drinks firm. So a quick walk to speak to the manager on site, and tell him of the situation, and two minutes later up turns a fork lift truck with three dozen cases of soft drinks! I must admit it went down a treat with everyone including me. Apart from dealing with two firemen with slight cuts no one was taking off to hospital.

Another big fire involved a night club in St. Albans, Graham the ambulance officer who was on call lived just across the road from the club, apart from a long drive leading up to the grand old house, in which the night club is situated. He arrived and asked for my assistance because of the number of clubbers involved. By the time I arrived there were hoards of young people standing around as more and more fire appliances were arriving on the scene. The fire had taken hold and was spreading very quickly. The young people had evacuated from all the various fire exits and it was a job getting the people to go to the main car park out of the way and for their own safety until the number of fire appliances had arrived. It was an extremely cold night, and the girls especially were only scantly dressed, so we had them sitting in our staff cars and in the one ambulance we had to keep them warm. The trouble was several hundred wanted to get in our vehicles!

Once the police were satisfied that the scene was clear enough of fire appliance movements, they led all the clubbers down the drive onto the main road so that taxis and parents could pick them up. Graham and I walked all around the burning building just to make sure no one had been left behind. Once that was done I went and left Graham and the ambulance crew to it. We went back to where our vehicles were parked and found we still had young girls in cars keeping warm!

I attended numerous house fires where people had been burnt to death. The smell of a burning body hangs in the air and on your uniform, even though you go home and change and even when it is laundered it seems to stay around. At no time do we remove these bodies as they are left in situ for the police and the fire service to exam the scene. Several fires, where fireman had been injured, they had to be taken to hospital. Three firemen who went to a house fire involving five children who had been overcome with smoke were injured as they rushed into the house to rescue the children, all involved were treated and sent home afterwards from hospital. Another two had been overcome with smoke inhalation and cuts to their arms as they tackled another house fire. One other involving a factory where a worker had started to tackle the fire but fell over and broke his leg and the fireman that carried him out of the burning building also slipped and both of them were taken to hospital. .

Unfortunately during my years in the service I attended three funerals involving the deaths of firemen. The first one was a big factory fire where a wall had collapsed on a fireman killing him.

The other two involved two firemen enroute to an RTA in their Rescue tender. It was from Hatfield where they were stationed, going to the A505 near Baldock. As it approached the town centre of Baldock it had crashed into a roundabout killing the two firemen. I knew these two men very well as they nearly always manned the Rescue tender that was sent to some of the entrapments that I attended, they were a great team, as we worked together we all knew them by their first names.

When our service merged with Bedfordshire, my opposite number from that county had an arrangement with the Beds, police that they would give us an appreciation in dealing with riots. The police had the use of an old brick works which also had derelict buildings. One evening about six of us were invited to go to a riot training exercise. The police had a group of young people who were only to willing to throw bricks and stones at policeman, but police officers were the only ones allowed to throw the petrol bombs! There sense of humour only stretches so far. It was a very informative night for all of us. We all had petrol bombs thrown at us just to see what it was like if this ever happened to us, if it did then we knew we were too close to the action. Our role in any situation like this is to be nearby waiting for the police to bring the injured to us.

This was the case in Luton when several nights running, Bedfordshire police had to have extra resources brought in from Hertfordshire, the Metropolitan police and as far away as Sussex to deal with riots, mostly in the Marsh Farm area of Luton. We also had extra ambulances and officers were situated near to the area. Luckily our only role was to take away several minor injuries for treatment to the L&D hospital.

There were some further big skirmishes in Luton and the Dunstable area when England lost in the football championship. Several officers remarked how the Metropolitan police came into the area with only a small amount of their vans, and within minutes they had dispersed all the trouble makers.

I was approached by the British Heart Foundation regarding them supplying the police with automatic Heart Defibrillators. Would we be able to help in training the police persons who were going to use them? I thought this would be a really good idea.

The initial use would be limited to the Armed Response Units and to the Motorway units. These vehicles can arrive on the scenes far quicker than we can, and if it only save one person from dying from a heart attack, who would argue against that. I handed this training over to one of our local trainers. I am not aware of any of these units being used on any patient prior to me leaving the service.

In 1993 Beds & Herts, Police purchased a helicopter, and the Chief Constable approached our Chief to see if there was a possibility that in some cases it would be use to us in medical emergencies. Along with Tim and one of our trainers we went to Luton airport and met up with the Inspector and sergeant in charge of this unit. Having insured that a stretcher could be placed into the aircraft, and our equipment could safely be used without any detriment to the avionics, I got Tim to set up a protocol for its use. The only thing I stipulated was that only an officer could be allowed to be flown in it with a patient. This also allowed an ambulance to be freed up to convey other patients at the scene to hospital perhaps of not such a serious nature.

As the officer always had the use of a car, the policeman who was being left at the scene, could always make his way back to Luton Airport where the Helicopter was based. The protocol was set up, and our control as well as all the staff on the road, knew when the use of a helicopter could be called for and who was going to man it.

It was used successfully on numerous occasions in dealing with RTAs, mostly in Bedfordshire to convey patients that were seriously injured, and would benefit from being treated at a specialist hospital straight away rather than going to a local hospital for treatment and then on for specialist treatment at another hospital. The two main hospitals we used were Addenbrooks in Cambridge and The John Radcliffe in Oxford. This increased the survival rate of the patient significantly. It was a great success and it was nice to know on several occasions the police were visited by grateful patients thanking them for helping in their rapid recovery and from perhaps death.

I used them on two occasions, once to find a motor cyclist who was using his bike off road across open countryside. We had been called to a patient who had come off his bike in an area between Offly and Hitchin. The caller said he had made his way to a phone box to call us but was unsure where he had left his mate. It was only minutes flying time from Luton airport and didn't take long for the helicopter crew to find the patient who was not seriously injured.

The second patient was a little trickier to sort out. it was a beautiful hot sunny Sunday evening, Tim the officer on call was sent to a chalk pit out of the back and beyond of Luton, to an off road motor cyclist who had come off his bike and seriously injured himself. Tim had arrived in his little Ford Fiesta van and was able to get into the pit next to the patient but the ambulance was not able to get anywhere near because the terrain was a very narrow mud track. I was called to see if I was able to get my Frontera to the scene and convey the patient into hospital. Whilst I was able to get next to the patient in my vehicle, once loaded I thought it could be dangerous with the extra weight going along the very narrow track that had drops of over 50 feet.

We called in the helicopter from Luton and asked them if they could come to our aid. We found a landing area about 100 yards away from the patient which meant that we would have to carry him that far, as there was enough of us to be able to do it. The helicopter came in and had a look around and said over the radio to us that as it was a hot day, plus our location was below sea level, they would have to fly off to burn off some fuel, other wise they would be unable to take off with everyone on board when loaded. That being accomplished they came back to us and we loaded the patient on board but they took some time in taking off as I think the pilot was still trying to lose more fuel. I gingerly went back up the track, back onto the main road.

The police, like us had their fair share of accidents and assaults. One particular policeman based at St. Albans always seemed to be involved in some kind of incident.

Apart from seeing him at quite a few incidents we both attended, I was first called to him when he had been chasing someone, when the person got to his front door he slammed it shut into his arm that placed to protect him self and his elbow went through the glass window pane of the door. He had an almighty laceration to his arm which required surgery on at the hospital.

Not long after that he spun his panda car off the road and we carted him off to hospital again. But that was not the only problem, his personal radio had been lost, and this caused a major headache to the police. They searched his wrecked police car and the area where he had crashed the car, and then they asked us if we had seen it. We check our ambulance in case it was still in the vehicle. We searched it from top to bottom but we could not find it. They came and interviewed us and asked us the usual questions whether we remembered seeing it lying around, and did we see it on the policeman when we took him into hospital. No as an answer did not go down too well with the powers to be in the police, so they even came and searched our vehicle, and still they never found it.

One of the Motor way patrols Land Rovers overturned whilst going at speed to an incident on the A1M, we conveyed two policemen to hospital but luckily they were not too seriously injured. Whilst dealing with an accident on the M1 junction 9 to 10 the police had their Land Rover Defender with four blue lights on, plus the scene was conned, a car ploughed straight into them! The area was also well lit with street lights. It just shows what some moron motorist are like, we conveyed four policemen to hospital in three ambulances.

I remember one police inspector being asked by a ITV Film Crew who made a documentary on "Staying Alive on the M25" 'What do you think of the general motorist?'

'What do I think of the general motorist' he answered

'They are all lemmings, they don't look far enough ahead, and they live in their own little world and don't give a damn about anyone else, except themselves'

I also featured in that documentary along with my fellow officer Graham. We were called by control to a serious accident on the M1 near to junction 9 Northbound. We travelled from Garston station to find on our arrival that a foreign lorry had jack-knifed. The driver had been thrown out of his cab onto the southbound carriageway and had been run over by several cars.

"IF" is used so often but "IF" the lorry had been English, the driver would have been alive today, but because it was a foreign lorry he lost his life.

The tractor unit had jack knifed into his trailer, if the tractor unit had been an English lorry then it would have jack knifed and trapped the driver in his cab. Because it was foreign , it forced the driver's door open throwing the driver out onto the opposite carriageway. And "IF" he had been wearing a seat belt he would not have been thrown out of his cab. But as I say "IF" what a little word can make such a difference to life.

The documentary had used this accident as the closing part of the film and it was handled very thoughtfully and it showed up the rubber neckers who slow down and cause more problems for all the three emergency services at any scenes.

The Inspector who was asked on the documentary about drivers, we had a big shouting match at each other at one incident, but we ended up as best of friends. It all started at about 0600 hrs on the M1 junction 9 southbound, once again by Watery Lane Bridge. A lorry had been carrying chemicals and had a collided with several other vehicles. The on call ambulance officer was dealing with it until I booked on duty at 0800hrs, and I went to take over from him. On my arrival the scene had been cleared of all the injured, but the chemical lorry had to be unloaded by experts whilst the fire service stood by. The other big problem was all the trapped cars waiting in the queue behind the accident had to be released first before any unloading of the chemicals took place.

The fire service had been advised that the area should have an exclusion zone in case any one of the drums split open causing toxic vapour to the area. The Hertfordshire highways had to cut open the Armco barriers and put down hard core for the trapped vehicles to turn round back onto the northbound carriageway. Once that was all done we then had to wait for the chemical waste disposal firm to arrive

As all this was happening, several of the police were becoming unwell with breathing problems. They had all been there from the start of the incident and it was now about 1000hrs. As more and more policeman began to feel ill, I called in to control and asked for three ambulances to be sent to my location. By now we had ten policemen who had been taken ill. On arrival of the first ambulance I put three policemen in, that seemed to be worse for wear than the other six, and sent them on their way to hospital. With that the Inspector came after me like a raging bull and demanded that all of his staff should have all got into that one ambulance.

I could see he was not a happy chappie, so I took him around the back of the canteen wagon that had just drawn up whilst he was still raging at me. I told him that number one it would over load the vehicle, and number two if any one of those policeman collapsed on the crew member in the back or others taken worse he would have his hands full, number three you know we do our job well, just like you do, so now let me get on with it. He smiled gave me a big bear hug (he was a big man)

'Thanks for that I know you are right'

Ever since that day, it was great turning up at a scene because we knew each so well I even got invited to his retirement party. My son Andrew was doing another side line in making model white metal ambulances so I presented the inspector with a Beds & Herts Ambulance model. He had a good laugh at that and said

'Are you trying to remind of something?'

Getting back to the chemical incident I got a phone call from my Andrew asking if I was at an accident on the M1 involving a chemical lorry? I said 'Yes'

'Well I will see you in about 20 minutes, we are just waiting for clearance from the police to get on the motorway the wrong way to unload the lorry and take it away for disposal'

The firm he was working for were the only local firm which disposed of these toxic chemicals safely. So he turns up and says 'I have been told by the fire service to put on all my hazardous gear in case this all goes pear shape, don't they realise I deal with this stuff all bloody day and I know more about it than they do'

He went onto say 'We also brought or own chemist along, to insure that what is on the label is what it says in the tin'

'As you might have noticed that lorry has not got any orange plates saying he is carrying hazardous goods so he might be hiding some thing'

All day long as this operation continued a long stream of reporters turned up to interview the fire officer in charge and the police inspector, thank fully they never approached me even though I was next to these officers. I enjoyed my self in the sun protecting the canteen wagon! At the end of the day we had taken four people from the original RTA and ten policemen into hospital for a check up, all were released.

Another accident, involving a chemical lorry. This time at junction 9 of the M1 the exit slip road northbound junction with A5. I had just picked up my mum to take her my house to have tea, when a call came in to a tanker and school coach involved in collision. My mum was terrified as we drove at speed through St.Albans to get to the scene she kept saying 'You can drop me off here and I'll wait for you to come back for me!'

Two ambulances were already on the scene, as I arrived they were dealing with children from the coach. It appeared that what had happened was a Dutch tanker lorry had come of the slip road from the M1 failed to stop and collided into the side of the coach. We had four ambulances to deal with the injuries ranging from serious head to broken limbs. We also had two of our Patient transport double manned ambulances to take away the walking wounded. In all we took twenty children altogether to hospital. I was very impressed with the children involved, the senior boys were looking after smaller boys and they did a fantastic job in keeping everybody calm. In fact I was so impressed that I went to the school the next day and saw the Head Master and told him how I was very impressed by their behaviour.

When all the children had been taken off to hospital the police chief inspector came up and said I have just been over to the lorry to see what was leaking from the lorry, 'Well what is it Sherlock' I said,

'Its like gas' off he walked back to the lorry and talked to the driver again who tells him its stuff to put in natural gas to make it smell like gas, 'Ah well' said a sergeant 'That's why its smell like gas sir'

'I hate bloody clever sergeants' said the chief inspector.

Nothing more happened so I went home with mum. About a month later I saw the chief inspector from the M1 accident and just chatting away to him, he told me he ended up in hospital four hours later after sticking his finger into the solution and smelling it! I had a bloody good laugh at his expense and I said to him

'Well that will teach where you stick your fingers and sniff it!'

A405 Colney Heath long about a police motor cyclist had been involved in an accident. Whilst we were dealing with a sudden illness, I heard a call go out to our other crew. Gerry attended the scene, and we heard him ask for a doctor standing by on his way in to hospital. We had just unloaded our patient so we stood by to give him a hand. But unfortunately the policeman was declared dead on arrival at hospital.

A405 Bricket Wood, another police motor cyclist accident this time he was trying to stop a motorist, he knocked him off his bike. Having been on my way home I was first on the scene, the leg injury to the policeman was extremely serious. Within minutes the ambulance was on the scene but the paramedic was unable to gain access for a canula so we could set up a drip, so without wasting further time he was rushed into hospital. But unfortunately he had to have his leg amputated.

As I said earlier we attended most calls involving the police dealing with firearms. These jobs were either late at night or very early in the morning. We were normally involved in the operational talk given by a senior officer, then we would all make our way to the scene in a convoy

.

The police were telling us all were we where going to in Borehamwood, when one of the ambulance men said that we had dealt with that man several times before, and he hides a sword under his bed. The police inspector was very pleased to have this intelligence, because they were unaware of that. They were explaining that they were going to raid the house for guns. We were to be there, as precaution if any thing went wrong as they broke in.

Abbots Langley the police raided a house that contained cannabis, the chief inspector in charge asked if I have ever seen one, which I hadn't, so he let me get to the front door, the smell for me was over bearing and the heat from the lamps was also something I was amazed at. At another house raid, armed police took down the door to a house in Hemel Hempstead and frog marched out two males. It's amazing how quickly the police gain entry to the house and get the occupants out without any trouble. This was another raid, because of suspected drug and firearms.

Out in the fields in Codicote some male had run off from his house with a shot gun. It was late at night with no lights in the area as it is very rural. The police had the area contained in a lane off from the village. Two fire arm response units were waiting for instructions as to whether they could open fire if the need arose. Once that permission was given, they went off with night vision apparatus to look for this man in the fields. It took an hour to locate him, and he surrendered to the police without any problems.

Toddington service station on the M1, a policeman had serious facial injuries. I found a policeman who had gone to investigate a smell of burning on a coach wheel, as he got down on his knees to look the tyre, it exploded in his face, with serious consequences. I had to await the arrival of an ambulance to take him off to hospital.

CHAPTER 19:
The Royal Family and VIPs

Every time any member of the Royal family visited our counties we were notified by the police, and depending on the information they had at the time, they then had to judge if we needed to have a presence in the area they were visiting.

We always had to attend any landing site used by the Royal Family using the Queens Flight Helicopter. The Royal Air Force supplied the rescue and fire appliance every time, we supplied an ambulance and an officer, and we had to be out of view when the Helicopter landed or took off.

I attended the Royal Flight on three occasions, with Princes Anne twice and Prince Charles once. We had to be in attendance throughout the whole visit until the Helicopter took off

The Queen visited our counties twice by car but we only had an officer well out of view.

Not so when the Prime Minister, Margaret Thatcher attended our county, well that was totally different altogether. I turned up in my office at the usual time of 0800hrs to be met by the Assistant

Chief Ambulance Officer waiting for me. He lived in St. Albans anyway. I thought oh Christ now what have I done? I was told that whatever I was doing that day, not to, and get an ambulance crew you trust together now! You will then proceed to a factory in St. Albans where you will meet up with Police. You will be following Margaret Thatcher around all day. I was lucky that day as I had a good crew on, Dave and Gerry, and Gerry knew one of the policemen who would be escorting Mrs Thatcher around all day on his Motor Bike.

Our instructions on how to perform that day came from the police, we were to remain well back from all the police vehicles and keep up! Keep up?, bloody hell we had a Ford Transit that went from 0 to 60 in 17 seconds not a Jaguar, BMW Motor Bikes, or Vauxhall Carlton's that went from 0 to 60 In about 6 seconds. We followed her as she visited various places in the morning and then we were told she was off to Bedfordshire. We were instructed by the police to follow her to the county boundary, but no further, and be back at a location in two hours time to follow her again.

As we chased the entourage going towards the Bedfordshire boundary one of the police motor bikes was trying to get past one of the special branch cars and as we watched him try to overtake we were sure the car moved well out into the path of him to prevent him passing the Prime Ministers car. It was our friendly policeman Tony, and when we talked to Tony a bit later he asked us 'Did you see that special branch car nearly hit me?'

We said we did.

He said 'Apparently when you overtake these bods you have to give them at least ten foot clearance and they judged I hadn't'

The return of the Prime Minister in the afternoon went off with no problems, leaving us to return to our station congratulating ourselves on having a lazy day and being paid as well.

The biggest shock to hit this country for years was when the death of Princes Diana was announced.

The phone rang early Sunday morning and to my surprise it was my stepson Paul asking if we had heard about Princes Diana? Now for Paul to ring at that time of the morning and on a Sunday I thought he was going to tell me a joke, so I said

'No go on then what is it?'

'She has been killed in a road accident'

I just couldn't believe it nor could my wife. We turned the TV on and watched as the story unfolded.

Monday morning being the usual weekly prayer meeting with Chief, the death of the Princes was naturally mentioned. It was mentioned that there may be an involvement of providing ambulances on the day of the funeral service. We did approach various agencies to ask if we might be called upon to provide cover. We were told we had nothing to prepare ourselves for.

But by Wednesday that had all changed and an urgent meeting was called by our Staff officer to prepare for the funeral cortège to come through our counties enroute to the Northamptonshire Village where Princess Diana would be laid to rest.

Peter, the Staff officer for our service said that he had been contact with Hertfordshire and Bedfordshire police who wanted different arrangements within their counties to be carried out on the day of the funeral. Hertfordshire police only wanted our presence on the M1 motorway junctions, the only road used in our area on the day. Bedfordshire police wanted an ambulance to follow the cortège some distance behind up the M1 to the Buckinghamshire border. As the build up went on during the week towards the Saturday more instructions and meetings took place, because the powers in charge could see the national outcry coming from the British public and this was going to be much bigger than had original been planned. We decided along with police to have either a presence of an ambulance or an ambulance officer at every bridge and junction of the M1 throughout our counties boundaries.

The plains that were being used were the same ones that had been set out in case of the death of the Queen Elizabeth the Queen Mother.

We were told that that the police were expecting large crowds to line the route on bridges and in fields alongside the motorway and any advantage point that could view the cortège.

On the day, my wife and I watched the whole procession from the start to the outside of Westminster Abbey on the television. I was astounded by the huge crowds, to be honest I was not quite sure what to expect. After the coffin came out of Westminster Abbey I started to get ready to move off to my location at Junction 10 of the M1.as we had all been allocated a location and a set time. But it soon became apparent that these timings would be thrown out of the window. I don't care what people thought about Princes Diana, but no one could have expected what happened that day with the sea of crowds thronging the route, slowing the cortège down to a snails pace and in some cases stopping altogether.

Val and I left our house and made our way to the M1 at junction 9 to go to my designated location at junction 10 to meet up with the ambulance and Dave the officer who was to follow the cortège. I was dumb struck as I got onto the M1 there was not a single car on ether carriageway. The crowds were already lined up in fields this was astonishing.

A separate radio channel had been set up for the entire proceedings with Bob the Director of operations in charge in the control centre. I drove up to junction 10 and informed control what the situation was in my location. Bob told me to drive up and down to junction 9 and 10. If I say I saw forty cars on that day, and in the time frame waiting for the Princes to come into my area I think I would be exaggerating. The crowds just kept on coming,standing along side the motorway, and by the time I got back to junction 10 there must have been at least a thousand people standing on the bridge. This is a very large junction that has two bridges that go over the motorway, and I would say it was four deep in people all the way round it. Control kept every body up to date with the location of the cortege, and as it went underneath the bridges at our location people walked onto the carriageway to throw flowers onto the Hearse, it was astounding. But to me even more astounding was the few cars that were travelling southbound, and those that did, just stopped and people got out of their cars to watch the procession go past. It was remarkable I don't think I will ever see any thing like this again.

Dave and his ambulance had instructions to follow the Beds police car which would move off from junction 10, thirty seconds after the cortège went past the junction. Then the crowds started to disperse back to their cars which had been parked all around the area of the motorway but not on it. I was approached by a male person who had parked his car about three quarters of a mile away, he was having difficulty in breathing. He was having an asthma attack, and said if you can get me back to my car I will be ok as I have an inhaler in the car, which I did. It saved me treating him with my gear and I stayed with him until he was fit enough to drive. I must admit at first I thought it was a wind up because he didn't want to walk back to his car. I also gave a dressing and cleaned a wound to a female who had cut her hand on a fence as she climbed over it to get onto the motorway. Other than that all went well or so I thought.

That was until Dave phoned me after I had got home, he told me how he had got on or in his case not got on! After travelling three miles behind the police car one of the Royal protection police motor cyclist pulled up along side the ambulance and told him to leave the convoy to which Dave replied 'I have been instructed by Beds., police to be here'

'Well I am telling you to clear off or you will be arrested'

'I always think its nice to know where you stand' I said to Dave.

Dave went on to say 'I phoned Bob (Director) straight away and asked what I should do'.

Bob in turn got onto Beds, police control room and asked

'What's going on? don't you lot communicate with each other' as he explained the situation.

In the meantime time the police motor cyclist is getting to breaking point and as

Dave said 'Ah well' To the ambulance crew

'We had better slow down and pull into Toddington Service station.'

He went onto say 'I think the police motor cyclist was going purple under his crash helmet and I have no doubt he would have done something to us, if we hadn't gone away'

Bob then rang Dave and said 'No one at the police control room can talk to the motor cyclist, so you had better do what he has asked'

Dave said 'We've done that before you came back to us'

When I spoke to Bob later I asked him what on earth was going on with the police, can't they agree on plans that are laid down, or is it up to some little Hitler to change the rules as they go along. Bob said well its nice to know even the police get it wrong even though it was us who got the flack.

CHAPTER 20:
The Night Club Job

Finally, when I retired I went to work in a famous night club in Central London as a medic at weekends. I did this for a year, mostly working at weekends, now I thought I had done it all, but no this was one very big eye opener for me.

The club was, in my opinion quite well run, most of the security staff were men but we had one woman who helped me with the female clubbers, because when these people have taken drugs they can become quite irrational and can also accuse you of any thing. They also had undercover clubbers trying to catch drug dealers, which they had quite a good success rate of catching these dealers. When these people were caught they were always handed over to the police to deal with. It was my job to walk around the club every fifteen minutes to see if I saw anybody acting strangely, or asleep. I had to make sure they were ok if I caught them asleep too many times they were asked to leave by the security guys!

After dealing with ecstasy, cocaine or even heroin, which has now become the norm for ambulance staff to deal with over the past 15/20 years, imagine my surprise when I was first presented with a patient who had taken "K" (Ketamine).

Ketamine is a short acting but powerful general anaesthetic which depresses the nervous system and causes a temporary loss of body sensation. It is used by vets to knock out animals, including horses, and anaesthetists when operating on humans.

The effect from taking this drug can cause perceptual or hallucinations not unlike LSD did when it came out in seventies. It reduces bodily sensation and the trip can last up to an hour, some takers say they feel like they are floating.

This a list of symptoms that were presented to me when people had taken "K"

Physically unable to move, Panic attacks, unable to feel pain, suppresses breathing and heart function and unconsciousness. If the "Clubber" had been drinking or mixed it with other drugs it leads to high blood pressure. The trouble with these people or even their so called friends they would never ever tell you the truth of what they had taken, even when you presented them with the worst case scenario. This patient is going to hospital because I have called an ambulance because his/her condition is so serious that they could die. The response from "THE FRIENDS" either laughter or

'Christ what the fuck are we going to tell his/her parents'.

One twenty four year old female was presented to me deeply unconscious and vomiting I was struggling to find her pulse, and she was going into respiratory arrest. All her friends could say was 'She's going to wake up with a big hang over and wait until we tell her she was showing of her fanny of to every one'

They also would not stop laughing as they were also under the influence of something themselves. I couldn't get involved in all this crap. I was struggling to ensure she was kept alive until an ambulance arrived.

I got the security staff to take these moron friends of hers out of the way and write a list of what she might have taken. The LAS ambulance crew arrived in very quick time thank goodness, and I assisted them to get this young lady into their ambulance so they could start more invasive skills. The security staff handed me a list of stuff she might have taken. I was astounded, Champagne, Vodka, Cocaine, Heroin and Ketamine, no wonder she was at death door.

On one occasion I had three lads who had taken "K," given to them by their limousine driver as they had come up from Reading for a night on the Town. The first lad was already deeply unconscious and his mates could not understand why they were ok, as in their opinion they were ok. I knew different as I could see the signs coming, that they were also going under, and sure enough within five minutes the second one went down, then within 3 minutes the third. I had already got an ambulance on route to the club and up turns a LAS rapid response car. The responder was a pleasant guy who was not amused to be presented with two patients and then a third as this lad crumpled in front of him. He called for back up and also for three ambulances to the address. You can hear the response from the controllers as they inform that him he has another responder coming to his aid, and at that moment only one ambulance! When every body from the ambulance service had arrived outside the club it looked like a war zone. There were two response cars and three ambulances. The manager of the club who was outside looking at all the chaos going on turns to me and said 'Gordon you only had to ask me. and I would have given you free tickets for all your mates to get in'

My first aid room was locked on one occasion and as I looked through the window in the door I saw a very well known D.J. snorting coke along with a male and female friend. I thought I would give them another ten minutes and then go back to my room. I still could not get in my room, so imagine my surprise when I looked through the window again and I saw this DJ and his friend spit roasting the woman!

Another drug I came across was GHB Gamma Hydroxy Butyrate, basically it means it's full of crap! Degreasing solvent or floor stripper mixed with drain cleaner!

It can cause convulsions, stomach problems, breathing problems, muscle spasms or numbing of the muscles, respiratory arrest, unconsciousness etc, and has led to several deaths. It can be used as a date rape drug as it leaves the person disabled.

It is used more on the gay scene rather the than straights, as one clubber told me. I sent several clubbers off to hospital suffering serious effects of this drug.

One time I came across men taking photos on their mobile phones up ladies their skirts. These men were soon booted out by security guys. I also came across two men and a lady having sex against the wall! The male security guys took the men away but when it came to the ladies turn to be taken out by the female security guard, the lady was a bit slow to move off, so when asked what the problem was the clubber replied

'I've got to pull my knickers up!'

'Well you shouldn't have had them off in the first place' Hazel retorted.

We had a few punch ups, but nothing untoward, I missed the shooting and stabbing!

I enjoyed my little job there, it was very enlightening and the majority of clubbers were quite a nice bunch of various social groups.

Now as I come to the end, more than likely you have noticed the only time I normally did any work, or any thing worthwhile was a Sunday. So please you heathens out there, please just go to church on that day and stay in doors the rest of the time

I have also gone full circle. I have ended up working for my son Andrew who in his diverse mind owns two companies. A home for the mentally ill! My daughter Nicola is the manager. The other company he owns is a garage, car repairs, servicing, importing cars from Japan and car sales. I don't think you can get any more diverse than that.

When I am not running around for them, I work with an old work colleague (who I mentioned, was the young ambulance man on the M1 motorway accident with the awkward L/a, and the decapitation) He now runs a successful private ambulance company and that has brought me right back to where I started dealing with people. And some of these jobs have also been very interesting! But may be that's for another day?

Printed in the United Kingdom by
Lightning Source UK Ltd., Milton Keynes
138748UK00001B/67/P